CONSCIOUS
SUSTAINABILITY LEADERSHIP

CONSCIOUS SUSTAINABILITY LEADERSHIP

A New Paradigm for
Next Generation Leaders

Alfredo Sfeir-Younis, Ph.D.
Marco Tavanti, Ph.D.

Planet Healing Press

First Published in 2020.

Copyright © 2020 Planet Healing Press

Dr. Alfredo Sfeir-Younis

Dr. Marco Tavanti

ISBN-13: 978-0-578-69524-2

ISBN-10: 0-578-69524-3

Cover Design by Julie Tavanti

Figures and Illustrations by Marco Tavanti

Printed in the United States of America.

I dedicate this book to my son Alfredo-Alejandro Sfeir-Camarena. He is a true inspiration in my life and a unique leader for the 21st Century.

Alfredo Sfeir-Younis

I dedicate this book to my daughter Julie and to the young generations of leaders who, like Greta, strive for a better, sustainable, just and more inclusive world.

Marco Tavanti

Contents

Figures

PREFACE

The future of humanity needs new leadership paradigms. This book is a message of hope for long term-paradigmatic transformations in times of crisis. The COVID-19 pandemic emergency and global crisis has generated a crisis at multiple levels from health to social relations, and from economic productivity to common good leadership. This crisis should generate an opportunity to revisit our awareness on the meaning and purposes of our existence as well as our call to serve and lead for the well-being of our communities. It is a challenging time where leadership decisions and behaviors will be judged by their defense as well as the contributions to the well-being of people in the short, medium, long term.

Suddenly sustainability is revised and appreciated as the time for emergencies call for a reassessment on the root causes of pandemics and the socio-economic conditions that make some sector of the population more vulnerable. The recurring infectious diseases transmitted from animals to humans (zoonosis) highlight the imbalanced relations that human population has with its eco-systems of a common natural environment of a common planet. This crisis spurs us to revisit those relations often based on exploitation and economic greed instead of respect and integration. Infectious diseases scientists and environmental health experts remind us about the importance of planetary health. Human health is deeply interconnected to human development and the natural systems. That is why we cannot adequately prepare for pandemics unless we also need to address the effect how climate change, melting glaciers, deforestation, biodiversity loss, and extreme poverty are factors directly correlated to humanity's health, its well-being and its survival.

Now, more than ever, we need new paradigms. We need new paradigms for leadership as current and past practices often fall short to integrate long term and systemic solutions. We need new paradigms for sustainability as our planet cannot afford our current rate of consumption along with its unequal, inhumane and unsustainable ways of advancing economic development. We need new paradigms of ecology, one that is conscious of our interconnectedness and interdependence as people, planet and for our common prosperity. This book is about a new paradigm – one that envisions new directions for the next generations of leaders. It is about a new paradigm that connects leadership to sustainability while also aspiring to a deeper awareness – more consciousness. It's difficult to highlight this new paradigm if we do not talk about past experiences and models of leadership. Indeed, we cannot sufficiently illustrate these models and visionary paradigms unless we also connect to the current experiences and understandings of sustainability, development, values and management.

Alfredo's experiences and reflections on the many years spent at the World Bank and in its pioneering contributions to the field of sustainable development emerge here as a message of hope the younger generations of leaders. Marco's scholarship and systems thinking on leadership intersects with Alfredo's reflections to help give the reader a graphic context and visual representation of these complex subjects and crucial arguments.

The literature on leadership is multiplying as we speak. Each author appears to explain leadership with a new imagery or concept or association. Yet, most of the literature is still at the level of management and does not ask some of the deeper questions this book is posing to the reader. We can no longer accept half-baked recipes as our human existence yearns for more. We need new paradigms for leadership that recognize the interconnectedness of our human existence as individuals and communities, organizations and corporations, ecosystems and nature.

The first book I, Alfredo, ever read on leadership was the one authored by Dale Carnegie: "How to Win Friends and Influence People", published in 1936. Sometimes described as a self-help book, with more than 15 million copies sold worldwide. I ask myself today, how many leaders were enhanced from the existing books? If the books from Carnegie really transformed just one percent of those who read it, we would have at least 150,000 top leaders today, just from one book.[1]

Michael Shinagel, the longest serving dean at Harvard University (1975-2013), in his article "The Paradox of Leadership", states that "there are more than 15,000 books on leadership in print, and that articles on leadership number in the thousands each year. For him, despite the popularity of the topic, leadership remains a paradox. People who seek to understand it by reading a primer on the topic will inevitably be frustrated and disappointed. Leadership, after all, is an art, not a science. And leadership is not limited to a professional field or industry, be it corporate, governmental, military, academic, religious, or service. Leaders transcend the confines of a defining box".[2]

(A) Let us collect the most important statements:

- *Leadership remains a paradox.*
- *Leadership, after all, is an art, not a science.*
- *Leadership is not limited to a professional field.*
- *Leaders transcend the confines of a defining box.*

What paradox? What governs the art of leadership? Is leadership the same across professional fields? How do leaders transcend? What is the transcendental nature of leaders?

Joe Iarocci, on his blog 'Servant Leadership' states that "counting all formats, Amazon offers 57,136 books with the word "leadership" in the title. He offers 5 main reasons for this huge number: "many people feel free to offer opinions on leadership..., readers have many different tastes in leadership books..., anyone can publish a leadership book..., the practice of leadership is constantly evolving..., and there is no limit to the way leadership can be described...".[3]

(B) We could keep in mind two of those reasons:

- *The practice of leadership is constantly evolving.*
- *There is no limit to the way leadership can be described.*

What makes it evolve? Why aren't there limits?

Peter Bregman, in his article "Why So Many Leadership Programs Ultimately Fail", stated that "Every one of these leaders was smart, knowledgeable, and capable. They'd all read innumerable books on leadership, taken leadership skills assessments, and attended multiple training programs – including executive leadership programs at top business schools. They knew as much as anyone about leadership. So why weren't they leading? The answer is deceptively simple: There is a massive difference between what we know about leadership and what we do as leaders. I have never seen a leader fail because he or she didn't know enough about leadership. In fact, I can't remember ever meeting a leader who didn't know enough about leadership. What makes leadership hard isn't the theoretical, it's the practical. It's not about knowing what to say or do. It's about whether you're willing to experience the discomfort, risk, and uncertainty of saying or doing it".[4]

Bregman added: "the critical challenge of leadership is, mostly, the challenge of emotional courage. Emotional courage means standing apart from others without separating yourself from them. It means speaking up when others are silent. And remaining steadfast, grounded, and measured in the face of uncertainty. It means responding productively to political opposition — maybe even bad-faith backstabbing — without getting sidetracked, distracted, or losing your focus. And staying in the discomfort of a colleague's anger without shutting off or becoming defensive. These are the things that distinguish powerful leaders from weak ones. And you can't learn them from reading a book, taking a personality test, or sitting safely in a classroom".[5]

(C) Let us highlight a few points here:

There is a massive difference between what we know about leadership and what we do as leaders.

- *Every one of those leaders...read innumerable books on leadership.*
- *These leaders...have taken leadership skill assessments.*
- *These leaders...have attended multiple training programs.*

What makes leadership hard isn't the theoretical, it's the practical.

Responding productively to political opposition, without getting sidetracked, distracted, or losing your focus.

You can't learn them from reading a book, taking a personality test, or sitting safely in a classroom.

How do I find coherence between the knowing and the doing? Is it more important to be or becoming? Why should we seek harder and deeper questions instead of going for softer and easier solutions? Should we pay more attention to the practicality or the self-realization of a given vision? What is the main source of learning of a leader, knowledge or wisdom?

Also, after reading (curiosity) close to a hundred rankings of those whom are believed, or perceived, to be the 'best leaders' in the history of humanity, many, if not a good number of those cited are war mongers (Napoleon) who conquered the world killing millions of innocent peoples, or annihilated entire populations (Hitler), or made billions of dollars in profits. What is the yardstick?

It is surprising to see little or no mention of persons like Moises, Abraham, Krishna, Christ, Buddha, Gandhi, Martin Luther King, and Mother Theresa. This raises questions regarding the real meaning of what constitutes leadership, the fundamentals of what is a true and indisputable leader, and the nature and scope of the ethical foundation of how one defines a good (acceptable) leader or a bad (unacceptable) leader. The time has come to question the true meaning of a "top leader."

This is a moment when we must re-kindle and revise the most fundamental attributes and the foundations of "success" not superficially interpreted in relation to money and power but to values and benefits to humanity. In these perspectives, success is a 'self-realized-path', it is the path of consciousness, where the values embedded in leaders are states of being, at the core of the equation. We hope that the content and scope of the self-realization of these values and sustainability paradigms illustrated in this book will somehow enrich your views and daily life experiences, in any activity in which you are involved.

The fundamental ingredient of a leader is what surfaces to his/her self-realization process within all forms of decisions and leadership responsibilities. And the essence of this self-realization process is about consciousness raising of our human nature as interdependent sentient beings with a responsibility to make the world a better place (not worse) for the present and future generations. These paradigms and applied values should help you to rediscover your own self and define your role within the context of sustainable development with an empowered citizenship.   We call this "The Consciousness Sustainability Leadership Paradigm (CSL)". This book is about the Conscious Leader.

PROLOGUE

"The fact that there is a beginning or an end is just a concept seeded into your mind by society. You are constant, continuous, infinite energy, and energy never ends, it transforms." –Anonymous

"In Africa there is a concept known as 'ubuntu' - the profound sense that we are human only through the humanity of others; that if we are to accomplish anything in this world it will in equal measure be due to the work and achievement of others." –Nelson Mandela

"The old Lakota was wise. He knew that man's heart, away from nature, becomes hard; he knew that lack of respect for growing, living things soon led to lack of respect for humans too." –Luther Standing Bear

LEADERSHIP IN OUR INTERDEPENDENT REALITY

Interdependence is a central element in most religious and spiritual traditions. We live in a new time of discovery of our interdependent identities. Although with numerous challenges and shortcomings, we live in a time of new paradigm emerging from the individual value of independence to the collective value of interdependence.

Pope Francis, in his encyclical, Laudato Si', reiterates how interdependence is a central reality in Catholic-Christian traditions: "God wills the interdependence of creatures. The sun and the moon, the cedar and the little flower, the eagle and the sparrow: the spectacle of their countless diversities and inequalities tells us that no creature is self-sufficient. Creatures exist only in dependence on each other, to complete each other, in the service of each other".[6]

In Buddhism, there is an explicit recognition and meaning of interdependence. It is essential to devote life to benefit others through love and compassion, and make an effort to diminish their suffering.

Several of Buddha's teachings have stated that: "Whatever exists has causes and conditions, and what does not have causes and conditions does not exist."[7]

Today, we live in a truly and fully interdependent reality in almost everything we do, we have, we are, or want to become. Thus, it is not easy to define pure causality over any phenomenon we observe or experience. We are realizing that everything depends on everything else. Nothing has independent or intrinsic existence although we are limitless-collective-beings, both over space and time. We live in a world of no boundaries or frontiers. This collective existence includes human beings, all sentient beings and (mother) nature.

This means that there is not just one cause or one condition to explain a phenomenon.

In the academic world, this inter-dependent reality is often expressed by advocating a "holistic approach" to the analysis and evaluation of any given reality or decision.[8] Holistic, in the sense that everything and everyone must be considered in one form or another. However, it is essential to understand that in a holistic approach, all the possible 'parts' of a given whole are interconnected, and the parts only make sense in relationship to a given totality (whole).[9] Today, our planet and humanity form a one collective reality, acquiring a very important role because it is difficult to separate 'this' from 'anything else'. We could conceive the planet as the container and humanity --including all sentient beings-- as the content. The content and the container as two inseparable beings.

The nature and experience of interdependence is defined and guided by our levels of consciousness. Higher levels of consciousness give us the experiences of the realization of our holistic-interdependent identities, which encompasses a physical, intellectual, emotional and spiritual experience. It is through consciousness that we attain the self-realization that we are both content and containers, both parts and whole of an experience that goes beyond our times, our contexts and our-selves.

Holistic Dimensions of Consciousness

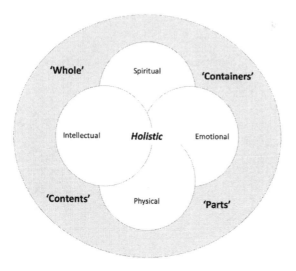

Figure 1: Holistic Dimensions of Consciousness

What does this mean in relation to leadership and sustainability? In a general sense it means realizing our interconnected and interdependent realities as human beings and sentient beings. In a very practical sense, it means that my personal welfare is also dependent on the welfare of all. In a universal sense, one could articulate this interdependent reality by saying "I am because You are, and You are because I am".[10] This self-realized interconnected and interdependent reality, in the way we experience it in our lives and on this planet, leads to different types of relations which we institute among ourselves (people), in socio-political-economic relations with each other (prosperity or poverty), and in the ecological and ecosystems relations (planet). In a leadership sense, higher levels of consciousness shift the nature of interdependence from a relation of dominance and ego-centered leadership/management (ego-leadership), into a meaningful and mutually beneficial ecological and ecosystems relations (eco-leadership), within which one is able to recognize the collective nature of our responsibilities toward all forms of life (seva-leadership).

Content-Container Paradigm Shift

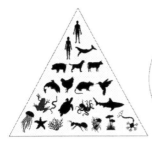  

EGO-LEADERSHIP
*Economic Development
with Dominance of
Nature*

ECO-LEADERSHIP
*Primacy of Nature
without Economic
Development*

SEVA-LEADERSHIP
*Sustainable Development
with Social Responsibility
and Ecological Stewardship*

Figure 2: Content and Container Relations of Humanity with Nature

The challenge is to go beyond anthropocentric views and practices of all our relations. It is also a challenge to recognize our interdependent existence with all experiences of life (organic and inorganic alike) but also beyond an eco-centric approach. It challenges us to embrace our existence into a relation based on the self-realization of love, wisdom, interdependence, respect, service and co-existence. This process of self-realization establishes the ground for understanding our planet as a living being and not just a thing.

This is a challenge to all those who aspire to be leaders in this world. With nearly 8 billion people on this planet, it is evident that we have to move from the "I" to the "We". The realization that we are one-inseparable-whole is now (i) embracing, for example, a new definition of how we conceive the nature and scope of traditional socio-economic development and (ii) structuring the processes of material and spiritual welfare of all beings. Moving to the "We" demands renewed attention to the new processes of wealth creation, human transformation and forms of wealth distribution at the collective level.

Going back to the theme of "causes and conditions", we should note that during the past decades we observe a lot of academic work emphasizing greatly the importance of 'behavioral variables' –to predict development outcomes. These are, sometimes, referred to as the human factor.[11] The human factor, which entails many ingredients, is seen as a fundamental cause and condition, which provide useful explanations and strength in the prediction of a given phenomenon or life situation. This is often expressed by saying that what matters it is not only 'the hardware' of life (development as betterment of life conditions) but also 'the software' (sustainability values for quality of life); what matters it is not only the 'hard skills', but also the 'soft skills'; what matters it is not only 'more quantity', but also 'more quality'; what matters it is not only 'material solutions' but also 'spiritual solutions'; and so on. This is a major change in paradigm.

In essence, this book singles out and emphasizes in particular how 'leadership' and the 'leader' -two key ingredients of the human factor--have become one of the essential causes or conditions to facing global challenges and decisions regarding, for example, the natural and human environments, ecology and natural resources, and sustainable development. This is the purpose of the book.

We are aware of many other causes and conditions influencing outcomes, including the existing social and political institutions, such as governments, corporations, and citizens. This book separates the possible influences and potential impacts that 'leadership' and the 'leader' play in attaining sustainable development objectives and goals (e.g., the UN sustainable development goals, or SDGs) for didactic purpose only. But, as it is pointed out, the purpose here is not just about any form of 'leadership' or any 'leader' within the context of sustainable development. It advocates for a major change towards the *Consciousness Sustainability Leadership* (CSL) Paradigm.

This does not mean that economic, social, institutional, political...variables are not relevant in the pursuit of sustainable development, because, indeed, they are. It simply means we will focus mainly on 'leadership' as the principal intervening variable in sustainable development and human empowerment. Thus, we will explore the unique components and attributes of the 'human factor', with the special emphasis on those attributes embedded within 'conscious leaders'. It will also present various methods and practices to implement 'conscious leadership' for sustainability.

To carry out the above aims, the book addresses (i) the core elements and various meanings of 'sustainable development', (ii) the existing paradigms of leadership with their virtues and limitations as expressed in today's literature. We identify key attributes of leaders who are and will be facing sustainability issues and constraints be it within the public, private, or civil society domains.

The traditional literature on leadership is greatly influenced by, and it borrows a lot from, from the literature on 'business management'. This situation has led to confusion and endless debates, including the identification of attributes that are supposed to be intrinsic to both managers and/or leaders (e.g., listener, committed, resilient). Some academic work states that the attributes of leaders and managers are one and the same. For them, a manager is a leader, and a leader is a manager. Is this really so?

We draw a major distinction between leaders and managers. Managers might not be leaders and leaders might not be managers. It also raises additional questions regarding whether a leader is something innate (a leader is born a leader), or whether one could create and form a leader. This is not semantics, as it defines the content and scope of many academic programs and curricula within post graduate programs in various universities.

This book explores the nature and importance of given attributes of leaders, depending on the leadership paradigm that is being advocated. The analytical issue here is to check the existence and strength of the attributes in relation to sustainable development. At the conceptual level, what is advocated here rests on which particular definition (notion) of sustainable development one choses, and in relation to what is to be done to attain it. We hold the view that no society will be able to attain sustainability without the empowerment of its citizens. Empowerment and sustainability are inseparable.[12]

In general, sustainable development may be viewed as (i) a stage of a development ladder or sequence; (ii) a collection of values, with special emphasis to collective values; (iii) a bundle of all forms of rights (human rights, nature rights) and the right to development; (iv) a mesh of power structures based on the actual ownership and access to renewable and non-renewable natural resources; (v) a distinctive style of life on this planet (e.g., neutral carbon footprint); and (vi) a unique and powerful state of consciousness, where nature is not a thing but a truly live entity (conscious development).   There is a strong correspondence between each of these notions and the paradigm of leadership one is prepared to choose and the attributes of leaders one is ready to advocate.

Some may suggest that sustainable development is all of the above. However, the approach proposed here is made fairly explicit: development does not end with 'sustainability' per-se, but with 'conscious development'; i.e., a sustainable development with the inner and outer empowerment of people and sentient beings. Conscious producers, conscious consumers, conscious leaders... This new paradigm is supported and nurtured by the level and quality of human consciousness, and the consciousness of all sentient beings and the conscious of Mother Nature; all playing a crucial and interconnected role.[13]

This means that leadership is not about behavior only, but about the causes and conditions of behavior: consciousness. Different states and levels of consciousness will lead to different forms of behavior. Behavior is indeed a dependent variable. It is not just about knowledge, but about being and becoming.

BOX 1: ABOUT CONSCIOUSNESS

"Life will give you whatever experience is most helpful for the evolution of your consciousness." **Eckhart Tolle**

There are hundreds of definitions of consciousness, based on dogma, philosophy, science (neuroscience), and experience. Despite centuries of debates, analyses and definitions, by philosophers and scientists, consciousness remains a controversial and very difficult notion to define.

"Success is not the key to happiness. Happiness is the key to success." **The Buddha**

When we talk about 'development' and 'transformation', be it personal or societal, it is important to know what is happening in outer self, "outer ecology", and in our inner self, in our "inner ecology". Two interdependent spaces. Beyond our daily infinite thoughts, to focus on our consciousness brings us awareness of that important 'inner being (space)'. It is there where our reality is shaped, and where perceptions and feelings towards that reality are born.

"Consciousness is the birthplace of change." **Anonymous**

We know from "experience" that reality is never the same for different individuals. Everyone relates to that reality in different ways and forms, sharing different messages, expressing different understanding, and having different attitudes. All, to the same reality. Thus, we all interact with the same reality in different ways. We also experience reality with different "intensities" (e.g., calm and collected, angry and in despair). Also, the same experience may create pain to someone and happiness to another. Confronted with the same reality (e.g., the crisis of climate change), some will act immediately and others will postpone the decisions to act. How is this possible?

"No problem can be solved from the same level of consciousness that created it." **Albert Einstein.**

One reason for these differences is because of the way each of us connects to the inner and outer worlds is completely different. Many argue that these differences come from our previous experiences, even past lives, and backgrounds (culture, habits), our capacities and willingness to understand what is actually happening (attitudes, efforts), and our behaviors, beliefs, perceptions, and feelings as 'receptors' and 'containers' of those realities. The same thought could be processed like this: a given reality may become a source of conflict for one and the foundation of inner peace for another.

"Just as a candle cannot burn without fire, men cannot live without a spiritual life." **The Buddha**

The way we define our own identity is rather diverse. For example, as regards to the same statement –e.g., "I am", "We are", "You are", and "They are"—we know that people define these statements in infinite ways. Each definition, of what is perceived to be, surfaces from the mind. However, the different definitions will become a major source of differentiated awareness and decision-making, defined by each individual consciousness.

"The key to growth is the production of higher dimensions of consciousness into our awareness." **Lao Tzu**

The thoughts we have, the life we proclaim, the experiences we face, the culture we embrace, the outer environment we recognize, the ways we have lived our experiences with others, and the various emotions and feelings we hold, are all essential to the responses and decisions we make. The great depository of these elements is our individual consciousness. In particular, 'how' all of these are organized and filtered form the foundation of management, governance, and leadership. Thus, for some leaders the past may be more important than the present, for others the present may be less important than the future. For some managers, a corporation may be facing a deep crisis, while for another manager the corporation may be swimming in an ocean of opportunities. Consciousness is the fundamental ingredient of these differences.

"There are many paths up the mountain, but there is only one mountain." **Swami Kripalu**

Within this world of permanent variability and constant change (an ever-changing reality), there are some components which are universal and always present: deep silence and emptiness, intricate spaces of perception, constant state of awareness (with or without any given content), etc. This is consciousness.

"The real revolution is the evolution of consciousness." **Anonymous**

All living beings have consciousness. Human beings, sentient beings and nature have consciousness; they are not just inanimate objects (things, matter). Because there are different types and levels of consciousness, we have different forms and qualities of decision-makers and leaders. Some are very attached to the consciousness of objects (gross layer of consciousness), while others are deeply involved in different dimensions of a given reality (subtle layer of consciousness). Some leaders are attached to the "having" and "doing", while others are walking the path of "being" and "becoming". Some leaders live in the "what it is", while others live in the world of "what it should be (or it should not be)".

"The core of your soul. The center of your being. The higher consciousness of your mind. That is where the kingdom of love and peace begins." **Anonymous**

Something so simple, as to say "yes", requires a tremendous conjunction of elements, attributes, perceptions, attitudes, realities...which are different from saying "no". Going onto one direction or another (changing directions) is a very intricate process, very much determined by consciousness, where consciousness becomes the vertex (interaction) of "experience" and the "intensity" one lives through that experience. These interactions –experience and intensity--move "the compass" to a given direction of our process of transformation and development. In actual fact, this compass is consciousness.

"Control of consciousness determines the quality of life." **Anonymous**

All of the above is relevant either to address some transcendental question (e.g., "who am I") or to driving a car every day.

"Remember that your perception of the world is a reflection of your state of consciousness." **Eckhart Tolle**

Consciousness is what gives meaning to the different experiences of reality. This capacity to give meaning to reality, establishes the grounds to reaching ever higher levels of existence, and understanding of that existence. We do not live within a nonconscious process of perception. That would imply to face a form of life that is without meaning.

"We do not see things as they are, we see them as we are." **Anais Nin**

This is why consciousness may also be defined as the "state" or the "quality of awareness" of our inner and outer reality. A fundamental state is that of 'being aware of oneself'. But this awareness must go beyond the self: all beings and nature (everybody and everything) --BREATH. In each state, we add to our individual and collective awareness, and we live this awareness with different levels of intensity --DEPTH. All, it becomes an experience, which agglutinates many forms and aspects of perceptions, feelings, emotions, memories, energies...belonging to our internal and external realities.

"If you light a lamp for somebody, it will also brighten your path." **The Buddha**

In a materialistic world, like the one we live today, for many people, matter seems to be more important than consciousness. In our view, consciousness is more important than matter, because it is our level of consciousness that gives sense to matter. This is not just semantics. The material evolution of a human being is not the end of the story.

"It helps to remember that everyone is doing their best from their level of consciousness." **Deepak Chopra**

There are different "types" of consciousness; e.g., individual consciousness and collective consciousness. Examples: 'consciousness that I am conscious' (identity, have an origin), 'consciousness that I am matter' (material, have a human body), 'consciousness that I have senses' (feelings, emotions),' consciousness that I grow, develop and move' (time, space), and 'consciousness that I am interdependent' (holistic belonging, co-existence). Also, there are different "states" of consciousness: the consciousness of being sleeping, awake, to cosmic consciousness (that we are part of a rather huge totality).

CONSCIOUS LEADERSHIP AS ECO-MORALITY

This is why we conclude that "Conscious Sustainability Leadership (CSL)" is a "space" and the "road" towards attaining higher and higher levels of consciousness and awareness: of oneself, nature and the essence of our spiritual reality. By focusing on consciousness, we are sending an important message: That the intrinsic characteristics of leadership are non-material (or beyond material as we know it), while its practice is launched within the material world. The non-material character of 'leadership' brings into more prominence the spiritual dimensions of sustainable development as well as the spiritual nature of leaders—i.e., the conscious leader.

The greatest attribute of a "Conscious Leader" is to transcend and contain ever higher levels of individual and collective consciousness, of himself, others, and nature. No great leader exists as separate from nature, and separate from the consciousness of nature. In essence, leadership is the result of the interplay among the consciousness of human beings, sentient beings, and nature. It is not knowledge but wisdom. It is not external but internal. It is not mental but spiritual. It is not individual but collective. And, so on.

Without this understanding, it is certain that many goals and objectives of development and human transformation will be left unattended or never fulfilled. For example, the UN SDGs will never be attained unless the individual and planetary consciousness raises. This raising of consciousness will translate into a different human behavior towards nature. Many of those SDGs demand the self-realization of human or nature's values, one of which being the value of interdependence. Other relevant values are cooperation, solidarity, justice, equity, love, and compassion.

The CSL will establish the ethical grounds for a new economics and politics, and the fundamental constructs of a new Eco-Morality. The Eco-Morality of total inclusion, understanding Planet Earth as a living being, considering all sentient beings, and respecting the whole creation.

A new path demands a new consciousness. The old consciousness does not have the attributes and mechanisms to create such a new path. This is not only possible, but this is a major human imperative for the benefit of all generations to come.

BOX 2: DID YOU KNOW?

SOME CURIOUS SUSTAINABILITY FACTS

Did you know... Google has a Vice President for Mindfulness? The role of VP Chade-Meng Tan as the head of mindfulness training is to enlighten minds, open hearts and create world peace. He believes that, as last century made us realize the benefit of physical exercise in our work and relations, the 21st Century shows us the scientific evidence of the benefits of the Buddhist practice of mindfulness and how it can be instrumental in catapulting it into the very heart of the business world.

Did you know... Most theories of consciousness come from religion and cognitive science including philosophy, psychology, neuroscience, linguistics, anthropology and artificial intelligence? Recent evolutionary biology theories consider the origin of consciousness in relation to the evolution of species.

Did you know... Material-ordinary matter (atoms) in the universe only comprises 4.6% of its total? The rest is dark energy (71.4%) and dark matter (24%).

Did you know... Our human body is interdependent with bacteria? What is known as human microbiome includes many resident microorganisms that play a vital role in human health. Our human body contains trillions of microorganisms with some estimations outnumbering human cells by 10 to 1.

Did you know... about a million people die every year from mosquito bites. That is about 2,700 per day, or 100 every hour. Mosquitos that carry the virus that causes Malaria is what causes most deaths. A child dies every 30 seconds from Malaria.

Did you know... The idea for the Sustainable Development Goals (SDGs) came from the Rio+20 Summit in 2012 when Columbia and Guatemala proposed a set of new goals to follow up on the Millennium Development Goals which were set up in 2000 to halve poverty by 2015. The 17 SDG goals include 169 targets, 234 indicators and represent five pillars: people, planet, prosperity, peace and partnership to be achieved by 2030.

Did you know... The United Nations Global Compact (UNGC) includes 13,000+ participant organizations, composed of roughly 9,000+ companies and 4,000+ non-business entities including 600+ academic institutions. They all make a principled commitment for sustainability for the respect and promotion of human rights, labor rights, environmental rights and anti-corruption.

Did you know... The movement toward sustainability reporting and socially responsible investing is growing exponentially? The Global Reporting Initiative (GRI) has been growing steadily since 1990 with almost 23,000 standardized sustainability reporting. Companies that incorporate Environmental Social Governance (ESG) continued to grow at a strong pace with about triple the assets identified in 2016 and almost 90 percent increase in the number of socially responsible investment funds.

CHAPTER I:
OVERVIEW ON CONSCIOUSNESS LEADERSHIP JOURNEYS

"You are not a human being in search of a spiritual experience. You are a spiritual being immersed in a human experience." –Pierre Teilhard de Chardin

"Consciousness is only the surface of the mental ocean." – Swami Vivekananda

"I think we have a duty to maintain the light of consciousness to make sure it continues into the future." –Elon Musk

"The great attribute of a leader is to transcend and contain levels ever higher of individual and collective consciousness." –Alfredo Sfeir-Younis

THE NECESSARY ALIGNMENTS

Since I, Alfredo, was a very young man, my teachers and friends often assigned me lots of responsibilities. At that time, my attitude was always "why me?" While earlier, I thought that I had become their slave, now, my perception of what happened has changed. Today, I firmly believe that they gave me those assignments because they saw in me some sort of a leader. Yes, I know that this term 'leader' needs to be carefully defined.

Today, I also notice that my tasks or where people want to see me making decisions are not just any form of assignments. They are different to those of anyone else's: director of an international organization, spiritual teacher, candidate to the presidency of Chile, running for the nation's Senate, high-level advisory activities, and more. None of these are some sort of trivial tasks. The "why me" has become more evident now, and the inner feeling of being a slave has disappeared.

To the activities assigned by others, I must add those activities to which I personally want to be involved. The tenor of my experience is as if I had an inner eye and inner voice which tell me either to 'get involved now' or to 'do not get involved at all'. And, when involvement is demanded, I do so, despite what I might feel or believe are my personal limitations. Over the years, I have come to understand much better this process –of activities and choices--than I did 60 years ago. It is clear that there are important causes, conditions, behavioral patterns, and human habits which are vital to keep my (our) inner life, memory and intelligence going. In many respects, this trajectory of past lives and present life have not been at all like a 'solo flight'.

This is a major inner alignment as a result of a higher level of awareness about me being or to becoming a true leader.

Similarly, I have been conscious that people did not ask me for any given task because of my personal attributes or glamour as a 'manager' (or administrator). While I believe that I am a good manager and administrator, coming to this juncture in life, most people want my leadership attributes and skills. I know from experience that 'leaders' and 'managers' are two different creatures; despite the fact one may find that some managers may be good leaders and some leaders may be good managers. But, in their essence, these beings are not one and the same. Leadership and management are not interchangeable concepts, functions or attributes. This is a major issue addressed in this book.

This is a second major inner alignment and awareness when structuring a discussion either about leadership or management.

All in all, I have no doubt that, in these alignments, my internal soul-searching process has played a fundamental role; what I call here my "spirituality" or my "consciousness". Spirituality understood not as simply a vehicle, a motivation, and an energy to get where I am supposed to go in this lifetime, but also as that unique inner space, and unique road to be travelled, necessary for the self-realization of values (with special emphasis on collective values), and for the inner transcending of my immediate material reality.

In the spiritual realm, it is as if there is a special process of softening the heart, opening the mind, and consolidating the path of transformation, all at the same time. To lead is not just another adventure within this material world. It is not something whose density and hardness are such that all is mechanical in our daily life.

It is central to align with the fact that most of the vital intake of management and leadership is non-material (e.g., solving problems and predicting the future). And, the processes we choose, in order to get where we would like to go, are also non-material (e.g., collective participation, human empowerment, with self-confidence, commitment, resilience). These non-material dimensions have given identity and validity to two essential ingredients in one's life: (i) wisdom as different from knowledge and (ii) intuition as different from rational thinking.

This is a third vital alignment with its awareness to understand the life of a manager or a leader, and the ways to sustain the right forms of leadership.

In my experience with assignments or activities I want to get involved into, leadership is not something that translates into: "I have to do everything", "I have to know everything", etc. Leadership and management are an instance where one experiences all forms of interdependence and diversities –with other human beings, sentient beings and nature. The best leaders in the field of sustainability will be those who are conscious, aware and self-realize all those forms of interdependence. This will enable the surfacing of processes within which all our relationships and interactions do not become a source of confusion –or, leading to competition, fear, falsity, and exclusion. On the contrary, they must become a source of happiness, self-realization and total transformation. This is the state of play where there is no need to fear about the other, or to bring-up our ego as a militant force of transformation. The transformation of the lonely "I" becomes the peaceful and graceful transformation of the "We". To understand this reality is vital to future leaders and managers. As a matter of fact, depending on where we are within this spectrum (between the "I" and the "we"), will be the style of management or leadership one will adopt.

In addition, we have to come to the clear realization that management and leadership are exercised within diverse and multi-nature environments. We are all different but, at the same time, we are all inseparable. This is when we learn that true life on this planet is a beautiful mosaic of infinite diversity. Thus, this is why the outcomes of any human activity will depend on actions by myself and by everyone else, at the same time.

This is the fourth vital alignment and awareness of the "other", because in management and leadership there is always another being and nature.

There is no universal trajectory of self-realization and the attainment of higher levels of human consciousness. For illustrative purposes, one may recognize, for example, that this trajectory may start with the core experience of the "I" (self) encountering the "Thou" (others) and embrace the experience of diversity as the identity of our being as a collective "we" (all). In such a journey one is more aware of the self-otherness, in which we become aware of the leadership responsibility toward others, humanity, sentient beings, and the universe (leadership awareness). This realization will in turn expand the realization of interconnectedness (sustainability leadership), and ultimately projected into a higher dimension that has to do with the realization of a "greater totality" (spiritual consciousness) as spiritual being with transcendental values and aspiration for a yet-to-be discovered cosmological destiny.

Levels of Consciousness

Figure 3: Self-realization levels for leadership, sustainability and consciousness.

MY INTEREST AND EXPERIENCE

From Alfredo: My interest in leadership, the leader, and in leading awakened several decades ago, when I saw with my own eyes the unique and indispensable role the 'human factor' plays in social, economic, and institutional development. I always knew that it was this human factor the fundamental intervening cause and condition of success or failure. Thus, if one studies either success or failure in socio-economic development one invariably sees that all depends, primarily, on that human factor, and not on the hardware of the development process (e.g., technology, infrastructure). Success or failure have a face, have a body, have an intelligence, have a behavior, have a memory...have life. Success and failures are life-entities (e.g., me, you, people, entrepreneurs, public servants, teachers, laborers, owners, managers, leaders...)

My studies and practices of, for example, Hinduism, Buddhism, Judaism, Taoism, and Christianity have shown (i) that there are different and alternative foundations of leadership --as a paradigm or function; (ii) that no one leader is the same, and (iii) that no style of leadership embraces the same attributes. To depart from traditional approaches to management and leadership, I wrote three small pieces (i.e., The Tao of Management, The Tao of Politics, and The Tao of Leadership) showing how different Taoism is as a conceptual framework; be it, in leading corporations, governments, and civil society organizations. All of that has greatly shaped my notions of management and managers, and of leadership and leaders, and the relationship between the two.

As far as my professional life is concerned, I have devoted most of it to the overall theme of sustainable development; a theme which will be addressed in detail within this book. The preoccupation for ecology, environment and social transformation. It seems that the theme of sustainability has shifted the grounds of the debate on leadership   and   on   alternative,   or   opposing,   leadership paradigms. Many scholars are involved in restructuring the function or expected attributes of "leadership", in order to create new opportunities to attain the objectives and goals of sustainable development; locally, nationally, regionally or globally. In other words, the attention and the priorities to identify, or form, leaders who will be able and willing to address the many issues and challenges of sustainability.

Although this work will address several aspects of leadership in general and will present the counter proposals (including those of business management), the major emphasis here will be in changing and improving what is now known as the "Sustainability Leadership Paradigm". Thus, this book addresses mainly the necessary structural improvements of "Sustainability Leadership (SL)", and it proposes a new paradigm: "The Conscious Sustainable Leadership (CSL)".

The views expressed here are based on the general literature, complemented by my own personal, professional, and political experiences, as I have led many national and international exchanges on sustainable development for the last 50 years. Also, they are based on my spiritual development, challenges, and realizations.

From Marco: The interconnected notions of this book 'consciousness', 'sustainability', and 'leadership' reflect what I have experienced and learned in my last 30+ years of professional work. Consciousness, sustainability and leadership became three phases of my life. First, I started to work as a mechanical engineer and robot designer. This technical phase of my life was rewarding by becoming competent in innovative technologies and effective solutions for business. Yet, it also became less and less meaningful when I discovered people living in marginal and difficult situations in our society. Through civil service and voluntary experiences, I opened my eyes to new realities. I started asking myself if I wanted to spend my life just trying to make a profit or to invest my time and capacity toward something that held a higher purpose. As I experienced more service with the elderly and young people with different abilities and drug addictions, I became more conscious of my surroundings and the socio-economic situations of my community. I began exploring deeper meanings of my existence following Christian beliefs and Catholic values linked to Catholic Social Teaching.

This first level of awareness propelled me toward a second phase of my life – one dedicated to sustainable development, poverty alleviation and human rights work. During those years of my life I collaborated and worked for nongovernmental organizations, community-based nonprofits and faith-based organizations dedicated to better the life of informal settles (people living in slums), promoting and protecting human rights (especially indigenous rights) and providing opportunities for forced migrants and victims of human trafficking (including refugees). Ironically, these difficult situations showed me the meaning of life and provided me the experiences to learn international and sustainable development work. The third phase of my life coincided with my investment in academia and the study of value leadership. While remaining rooted in the values of service and solidarity with people on the margins, the call to leadership became a strong call to change things through systemic solutions. The first experience of serving people in poverty helped me greatly to solidify my values and my awareness to have a vocation in my life. This first phase was about discovering my awareness through interpersonal interactions and working with people from diverse backgrounds. The second phase of my life added to my discovery and deepened my level of awareness. I became more conscious through international and sustainability projects.

The third phase of my life has been an ongoing journey to seek systemic solutions to world problems through academia, cross-sector partnerships and leadership development solutions for professionals and coaching of seasoned leaders. The concepts and paradigms of this book with Alfredo represent some of the notions emerged from our reflective experiences through meditation for consciousness raising, through professional work for sustainable development solutions, and through leadership as service for others. While the ideas presented here emerged from our own experiences, the reflection models are intended to be relevant for everyone's journey. We hope these insights can help you to rediscover, advance and better articulate your own call to becoming a conscious sustainability leader.

CHAPTER II:
WHAT MOTIVATES ME AS A LEADER

"Make your work to be in keeping with your purpose" —
Leonardo da Vinci

*"If you want to identify me, ask me not where I live, or
what I like to eat, or how I comb my hair, but ask me
what I am living for, in detail, ask me what I think is
keeping me from living fully for the thing I want to live
for."* —**Thomas Merton**

*"Efforts and courage are not enough without purpose and
direction."* —**John F. Kennedy**

*"To live is to choose. But to choose well, you must know
who you are and what you stand for, where you want to go
and why you want to get there."* —**Kofi Annan**

Leadership is a call to serve. We may all have different calls
aligned with our diverse sets of values, passion, skills and
competencies, but leadership is a call to serve a higher purpose.
While leadership may be expressed at different levels in society and
organizations, a key step for all is to discern our call and clarify what
motivates us to make a difference in the world.

Alfredo's Mission: My mission in this lifetime is to heal the
planet. It is my conviction that leadership is one of the important

vehicles of healing. It is not only technology, production, trade...that matters, as portrayed by the present development paradigm.

Thus, it motivates me to change the world and change it now. To change the world through a new form of leadership. Also, the deep environmental and ecological crisis we are living today, brings to the fore this notion of sustainable leadership, and the formation of leaders for sustainable development. I believe that there is a common ground to explore together.

What motivates me to enter the debate on Sustainable Leadership (SL) is to see clearly how leaders for sustainability and SL may contribute to healing the planet. Global warming and climate change, biodiversity depletion, rapid desertification, shortages of water, pollution everywhere, ecological imbalances, contamination of the oceans, urban congestion, loss of natural forests, etc., are just some of the symptoms and realities in need of immediate healing.

What motivates me is to address comprehensively how leadership fits into the definition of strategies and programs to heal the planet. What are the types of leadership which will truly contribute to healing the planet?

What motivates me is to bring a new SL model that accounts for the relative importance of "the human factor", in all its manifestations. This opens a very different avenue for future debates. In particular, to contribute to the great importance of improving this human factor through higher and higher levels of human consciousness. Thus, I want to bring to this debate and our attention onto the relationship between human consciousness and SL, so that we heal the planet. In the proposal made here, human consciousness is the most important intervening variable, be it individual consciousness or collective consciousness.

What motivates me is to bring full awareness to the fact that the above diagnosis on the planet's need for healing is not new. It has been presented, debated, and advocated a million times at the local, regional and global levels. Something is to change now. For this to happen, it behooves to ask ourselves whether we should be 'doing more of the same'. Clearly, the answer is no, because more of the same will yield more of the same, and millions of us are not happy with the state of our planet.

What motivates me is to share that, at present, we are subject to a collective inability to heal the planet. This shows the great failure of existing leaders and the different forms of leadership.

What motivates me is the support to new leaders who are not only conscious of the need to heal the planet, but they are also conscious of themselves (i.e., self-realized beings). Conscious that, in the past, the key constraints were technological in nature and that, in today's world, the major constraints are ecological in nature (environmental, biological).

What motivates me is to genuinely find an effective and strategic path to be followed. For the moment, we are all witnesses of how existing governments, corporations, citizens, global institutions, governance, technologies, knowledge, etc., are incapable of finding and committing to the right actions. Today, we see actions which are not commensurate with the depth, urgency, and scale the situation demands.

If one were to ask a large audience for suggestions regarding what to do now to heal the planet, there is no doubt that many ideas will be expressed with regard to a new vision, mission, governance, policies, programs, investments, incentives... However, without taking fully into account 'the human factor', none of those instruments will yield the desired results. To travel the road towards healing the planet, it is very necessary and essential (i) that our global-collective-consciousness rises, (ii) that our consciousness creates a deeper and an expansive awareness to realize what is actually happening to our planet, and (iii) that our consciousness identifies what are the most appropriate solutions.

What motivates me is to bring more attention to the role played by human awareness, mindfulness, and different techniques of meditation. Without a very high level of human awareness nothing is really going to happen. Thus, leadership must be (re)connected to consciousness and human awareness. Something that the existing literature has done little about. This is why within the debate about SL, it would be essential to determine how we should create such individual and collective awareness and consciousness. Clearly, teaching, communications, and advocacy play a vital role in raising awareness. This would include the important contributions that social media makes. Nevertheless, and judging by the results, these instruments of communication have shown not to be enough. More information is not necessarily enough. More information does not necessarily lead to the right actions, behaviors, or efforts. I insist, again and again, that we need to find out more about the secret ingredient.

What motivates me is to see forms of leadership that bring important elements of success. In my career as a natural resource economist, I studied for more than a decade (1985-1996) the development performance of policies, projects, and programs (macro, sectoral and micro) within the developing countries (approximately 2000 completed operations). It is my experience that behind any given success in development, and sustainable development-e.g., the key to that success-- there is a person (a leader), or a community of interest (many co-leaders). My ex-post evaluation studies show, time and time again, that even if one could have the best technology, the most powerful ideas, or the most efficient delivery systems, in the end, it is the quality of that human factor (consciousness and leadership) the one that makes things happen. This is true of business management, marketing, design, implementation, accountability, transparency, technology applications, human rights compliance, poverty alleviation, social inclusion, and the like. In business management, something similar often happens. Naturally, the human factor performs differently or gets influenced by culture, vision, incentives, approaches, and methodologies used in management.

What motivates me is to become aware of how the literature on leadership has been influenced by a Western culture and a Western way of thinking. In this world management with the "m" of muscle. Only recently, Eastern based models are being given more prominence. In my recent books, I have proposed a different way to manage corporations, politics and citizenship. These propositions have been based on the philosophy expressed by the Tao The Ching of Lao Tze; not a Western paradigm of management. In using the philosophy of the Tao, it becomes evident that the nature, approach, and relevance of the human factor --and the collection of attributes associated with a 'good manager'-- are radically different. The differences between the Western and Eastern corporate management models have been the subject of a lot of controversy. To me, focusing on the roots of these different paradigms, the differences are so great that they are not even comparable or subject to linear contrasts. They are not to be conceived as extreme polarities and, thus, try to find a point in between. In this note, there is not much space to go deep into these controversies. One of my key objectives is to bring about the importance of the Eastern paradigm and how its essence will enrich the sustainable leaders and the SL. The literature really lacks comprehensiveness and depth of analysis. Lots of confusion still exists, and much more is to be done. Popular books about the habits of great leaders include mostly western leaders, in a western environment and within a western culture. Thus, the social grammar, which has been created to express notions of leadership, success, failure, human transformation, etc., has silenced so many aspects which I deem crucial for the future of the planet.

What motivates me is to confront many notions of success and failure. For many authors, these two situations are on the same axis; thus, success is the opposite to failure. Nothing further from the truth. They are two completely different situations, where the causes and conditions create realities that are not even comparable. As a result, many things are being left out. In some situations, if one is able to embrace failure in its totality, such failure may become a real success in understanding, in analyzing, in feeling, in behaving, and in deciding. What is eminently clear is that there is not one notion of success or failure.

Marco's Mission: My mission is to educate new leaders to become change-makers for the common good. My call is to be an educator through Jesuit, Vincentian and Catholic Social Teaching values that inspire me and others to center our values and align our actions toward higher-level benchmarks for human dignity, sustainable development and sustainable social impact. The discernment to understand our course of action and priorities in leadership is an ongoing process. The complexity of society, our institutions, our economic and eco-system relations are part of this discernment process. In the Jesuit's tradition, discernment is about integrating a deep-listening of dynamics that go deeper into a new level of consciousness – one that is embedded into spiritual and moral values that give meaning, purpose and reference to our leadership.

What motivated me to enter this field of consciousness for sustainability leadership is the encounter with marginalized sectors of our society, with people that did not have access to the level of dignity that should all deserve. These worldwide encounters have pushed me to take different paths and shift from a life of business only into a career for international sustainable development and poverty reduction. By working with Jesuit and other religious institutions that had a clear mission to restore that human dignity given to them by a common creator, I became motivated to go deeper in my discernment and dedicated my life to develop value-centered leaders.

CHAPTER III:
PART OF THE CONTROVERSY

"Management is doing things right; leadership is doing the right things." —Peter Drucker

"It is better to lead from behind and to put others in front, especially when you celebrate victory when nice things occur. You take the front line when there is danger. Then people will appreciate your leadership." —Nelson Mandela

"Do not look for approval except for the consciousness of doing your best." —Andrew Carnegie

"To lead people, walk behind them." —Lao Tzu

THE FRONTIER OF LEADERSHIP

At present, a lot of confusion pervades the debates on the Sustainability Leadership (SL): e.g., its content, scope, and derived policy recommendations within all levels of decision-making. This confusion surfaces from the concepts that are being proposed and the various interpretations as regards its proposed instruments.

Without a solid comprehensive explanation, most advocates bring to the fore too many badly defined complex dilemmas related, for example, to: (i) how one is to define who is a 'leader' and what is 'leadership'—i.e., two different aspects, though related in many important ways-- (ii) how one is to define the relative importance of a long list of issues (including some conceptual ones), and (iii) how one is to evaluate the different alternatives for the implementation of both 'sustainability' and 'sustainable development'.

We are fully aware of the thematic complexity of these four concepts -leader, leadership, sustainability and sustainable development. They have bloomed in all sorts of debates about: environment, ecology, global commons, morals and ethics, social inclusion, poverty and equity, justice and rights, democracy and participation, global goals and governance, the triple bottom line, international organizations and their global goals, the theory of capital and growth, issues of valuation, and the like.

Today, all of the abovementioned themes are packed very loosely into the term **SL**. This reminds me of the debates on "social capital" several years ago; in which every aspect of development was included in that form of capital. Part of the debate here will be essentially on how to unpack this debate.

Today, some defend the view that 'sustainability leadership' is really a new paradigm of leadership. This means a new and integrated approach to the identification and formation of leaders, and it is a path towards the practice of leadership within the realm of sustainable development. This paradigm is seen as different, for example, from those ones on leadership within the corporate world. Thus, we witness the development of some sort of 'anatomy' associated to this new leadership model, which is then compared to other approaches and proposals regarding the various foundations of leadership (e.g., the comparisons with such paradigms as 'corporate leadership', 'management leadership', 'organizational leadership', 'development-leadership' and others). Despite some limitations, I support the view that SL is indeed a separate paradigm. However, as this book argues later on, the way SL stands now is to be expanded and consolidated into a new dimension. The story about leadership does not end with the SL paradigm.

The Frontier of Leaders

Significant attention is being paid now to how a given society creates, trains, or conceives new 'leaders.' This is a very popular literature. They say that leaders are expected to be aware not only of sustainability per-se but, in addition, to be capable and sensitive to adequately address all issues surrounding "sustainable development".

The attention of this literature has been mainly on identifying important attributes, behavior, and habits of successful leaders (e.g., humble, honest, resilient, visionary, compassionate). Later on, we address several of these attributes, and propose new alternative ones, in response to the proposal we make about conscious leaders. These attributes are far and beyond those of corporate or political leaders.

For now, most of the attributes being advocated are seen as universal in nature. This is to say that the attributes in question would apply to characterize or evaluate any leader, anywhere, or to assess any form of leadership. This "universality principle" means that there are no unique attributes associated or embodied into sustainability leaders. For example, all leaders have to be honest and, thus, 'honesty' becomes a universal attribute of a leader, no matter what type of activity is engaged into, or no matter where he or she is leading (sustainability being one of those).

Today's literature reveals an intense competition among academics regarding who brings more attributes to the conversation. Authors within the SL field are now 'borrowing' at will from other paradigms (e.g., ontological coaching, business management). As developed later on, we conclude that much more research remains to be done on the uniqueness of attributes about the theme of sustainability and the search for new leaders and SL.

THE TRUE MEANING OF LEADERSHIP

Other authors are focusing much more on gaining a better understanding of the true meaning of "leadership", in or outside of sustainable development debate] -e.g., debates about "corporate management", "social corporate responsibility", "alternative forms of politics", "global public goods" or "international global affairs". Again, the aim is the same.

Let us focus for a moment on the debates within the realm of corporate management. There is a great deal of debate about the differences between being a 'manager' or being a 'leader'. Are they equivalents or are they the same? Some advocate that they are one and the same. Others advocate that they are very different in nature and functions. For example, Professor Warren G. Bennis suggests these are two different creatures, and he states that "leaders are people who do the right thing and managers are people who do things right". To us, this quote opens the door to even more controversy about leadership and sets the need for further discussions (e.g., the meaning of 'doing' and 'right').

More specifically, if one takes the traditional paradigm of "Social Corporate Responsibility (SCR)", the confusion arises when comparisons are made between CSR and the different notions of sustainable development, both at the corporate and global levels. CSR has been conceived in many different ways. In particular, CSR has been defined as a set of criteria, a bundle of policies and programs, a collection of values, a selected group of principles, or a different critical path to attain the aims and objectives of sustainable development within the corporate world.

Here we mention the corporate world, and not the government or citizens' organizations, because of the previously referred debate on managers and leaders. It would be through adopting a CSR approach that corporations could, in principle, make a significant contribution to a sustainable planet. This may mean to expand the scope of the term "responsibility" within the corporate world, specifically, and within the process of industrialization, generally. However, CSR is not the equivalent to sustainable development.

Responsibility v. Sustainability Dimensions

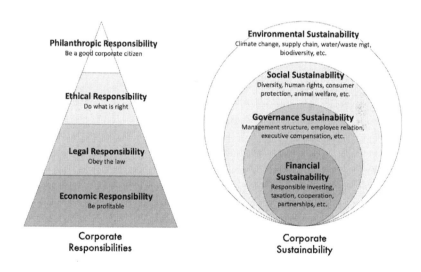

Figure 4: Corporate responsibilities and sustainability

The corporate responsibility dimensions are related but not equivalent to the corporate sustainability dimensions that are in relation to the environmental, social, governance (ESG) concerns and financial value creation through impact investing, cross-sector partnerships, and international cooperation for sustainable development impact investing. A corporate sustainability leader that is knowledgeable of these sustainability dimensions would need to be capable of incorporating them into the strategic priorities of the corporations at various levels. Consciousness is ultimately about the awareness and realization of what must be done, sustainability is about having an integrated notion of its environmental, social, governance and financial, human, spiritual dimensions and leadership is about the executive and efficient capacity to contribute to these processes at personal (values), corporate (performance) and global (impact) levels.[14]

CHAPTER IV:
EDUCATION FOR SUSTAINABILITY LEADERSHIP

"Educating the mind without educating the heart is no education at all." **–Aristotle**

"The consciousness of knowing how to make oneself useful, how to help mankind in many ways, fills the soul with noble confidence, almost religious dignity." **–Maria Montessori**

"Those truly committed to liberation must reject the banking concept in its entirety, adopting instead a concept of women and men as conscious beings and consciousness as consciousness intent upon the world." **–Paulo Freire**

"Education is the most powerful weapon which you can use to change the world." **—Nelson Mandela**

EDUCATION FOR SUSTAINABLE DEVELOPMENT

The United Nations has been on the forefront of promoting sustainability in the education of new generations and leaders. The UNESCO's Education for Sustainable Development (ESD) programs and connected initiatives have been instrumental for empowering academic institutions to educate people to develop appropriate mindsets and skill sets towards a sustainable future.[15] Since its inception in 2010, the United Nations Academic Impact (UNAI) is a growing network of more than 1,300 institutions of higher education from 130 countries committed to support and contribute to the realization of UN goals and mandate United Nations for sustainable development along human rights, access to education, and peace.[16] Even more inherent to sustainability leadership and management education challenges has been the contribution of the United Nations Global Compact (UNGC) that in 2007 launched a network of business universities and schools committed to the Principles of Responsible Management Education (PRME).[17] Today, the network of more than 650 academic institutions worldwide reflect a commitment of academic toward education for the Sustainable Development Goals (SDGs) and the 2030 Vision through responsible management and sustainability leadership education.[18] Commendable is also the Higher Education Sustainability Initiative (HESI), that emerged in 2012 from the United Nations Conference on Sustainable Development (Rio+20) which provides higher education institutions a platform to prioritize and share internationally their contribution to sustainable development across all disciplines of study.[19] In spite of these and numerous other emerging academic programs, courses and degrees connected to sustainability leadership, management and practices, we ask ourselves what is missing in these academic developments and educational approaches.

SOME TRANSCENDENTAL QUESTIONS

Given all of the above, some transcendental questions come to mind.

1. Is there a one-size-fits-all leader?

If this were true, there is no point in talking about a sustainability leadership model, because this would mean that the sustainability leader may be a leader anywhere in society. And the leader from anywhere in society may become a sustainability leader. This discussion brings about the issue of what defines a leader in sustainable development and about the "universality principle" in the definition of the attributes of a leader. Here, the view is that there is no one-size-fits-all leader, and the challenges of sustainability demands a special and unique leader.

2. Is "the core" of a leader and leadership, different, or the same, in different situations?

The 'core' is represented by how we define the architectural support and the anatomy of a sustainability leadership paradigm and a leader: content, values, skills, vision, behavior, empowerment... Thus, if one advocates that SL is singular and a unique paradigm of leadership, it is essential then to demonstrate that the essence of a sustainability leader is different from all others. This has not been done yet to the fullest extent, and we attempt to do this here. To identify the differences, if there are, in a satisfactory manner, it becomes the true 'acid test' we all need to pass.

3. What Are Universities Doing Now?

Some universities seem to have settled the above-mentioned issues and concerns. This is why today we see the blooming of university programs on SL. I must say that these educational institutions are not that different.

We ask ourselves if these institutions, and what they do and promote, are advocating in essence that there is a unique SL paradigm? Let us address this question via a quick analysis of their academic programs.

What we see is that the large majority of these programs are about training and enabling young people, or local communities, to address different aspects of sustainable development (e.g., social engagement, community empowerment, recycling, cleaning, planting). There is no doubt that such programs would create some level of awareness about the issues and the need for taking into account sustainability into development, be it at the local, national or global levels.

However, after studying the nature of those academic programs and activities, it is not clear whether the students who participate will, in fact, become real leaders as a result of these programs, or whether, later on, they would engage into SL.

One possibility is that these programs' implicit hypothesis is that one is not born a leader; that leaders can be made just with few management courses and specialized programs. Many of these academic programs assume that sustainability leaders can be made in vacuum without experiencing the reality of nature and sustainability. They also often omit to give a comprehensive, holistic and multidisciplinary education that is essential for sustainability leadership development.

However, there is yet another possibility, yet another implicit hypothesis: that these universities possess some sort of wisdom to hand-pick and select leaders within their programs and, thus, these programs are there to improve them.

We feel the universities are engaged in addressing the first hypothesis; otherwise, one would need to know the details surrounding the whole selection process. Specifically, if the students in those programs are naturally born leaders, then it would be interesting to do research on how the university defines the attributes of those leaders within the admission process. If they only admit leaders in those programs, what is their own definition of sustainable leaders? This is yet another important aspect of a complex puzzle involved in the debate on leadership.

There is a third possible scenario. It is possible that these programs are assuming that all of us have inside ourselves the "seeds of leadership" (something yet to be defined), and what these programs actually do is to provide a fertile soil and a clean water for that seed to germinate. This is a very important path to be followed; although, I see a black hole in the literature regarding the definition of that seed and how to make it germinate.

Thus, for the moment, we have concluded that just the fact that one learns more about sustainable development, or that one is more aware of sustainability issues, the programs of this nature do not necessarily make the participants a leader. It is very possible that these programs make them good and responsible citizens. And, this is an important achievement! I do not underestimate the importance of that.

It is clear that if we are to debate about leaders and leadership, one will have to go beyond just teaching and disseminating information (agreeing first on the right teachings and information). Given that, it is essential that these programs ought to have the methods and capacities to comprehend and self-realize the teachings and the information. This is not a question of knowledge by transformation and self-realization. The review shows that for the time being, the academic content of the above programs relates mainly to awareness creation in relation to a great plethora of sustainability issues, instruments, and practices; be them individual or community based (e.g., recycling, cleaning a beach).

However, will more knowledge on sustainable development – theory and practice—become a necessary or a sufficient condition to create a sustainability leader and, then, establish the grounds for SL? It may prove to be just a necessary condition, and certainly will not be a sufficient condition. And, it is on the sufficient conditions that we have to pay attention to in the future.

But, do not misunderstand me: those programs are indeed a vital step to attaining sustainability on this planet –as leaders or followers-- and to encourage people to get highly engaged. Also, these programs may awaken the innate leadership spirit within some of them.

THE WESTERN VIEW OF LEADERSHIP

Also, we see that most of these programs are based on a Western view of life, culture, ethics, human behavior, leadership, vision, mission, etc. Only recently, we begin to see an Eastern view of life, philosophy, cosmovision, ideas, and practices coming up, and be referred to, within the field of leaders, leadership, and sustainability.

Alfredo's Views: The interest in eastern spirituality made me, Alfredo, write about the Taoist approach to corporate management, citizenship and politics. The reference point was the Tao Teh Ching of Lao Tze. In terms of business management, the Tao structures a completely different manager and leader. Some of these aspects will be presented later on in this book.

Also, I have been a practicing Buddhist for many decades, and one of my purposes has been a special form of Buddhist spirituality: experiential and socially engaged (i.e., the spirituality in the public domain). Thus, the importance of embracing some spiritual principles to define and form leaders for sustainable development.

As I was educated Catholic, and I had a very strong curiosity for politics since I was a teenager, I read many of the fundamental writings of the church in such areas as peace, environment, labor, equity and justice. Also, I devoted time to read some Christian philosophers that greatly impacted the public domain (e.g., Pierre Teilhard de Chardin SJ, Jacque Maritain).[20]

I had a great teacher in Hinduism, particularly as regards the foundations of Vedic Sciences. A tremendous wealth of ideas, practices and attributes which are essential to understand our life on this planet.

Not less important, has been my studies of indigenous peoples' cosmovision and their implications for sustainable development. It is mainly from here that I have come to the realization that our Planet Earth is a live being. They are a tremendous source and inspiration regarding leadership and the attributes of leaders for this millennium.

I also have studied many texts in Judaism, Islam and other selected forms of spirituality.

For the moment, the literature is dominated by western views and prescriptions. The time has come to rejoin, and assemble a new paradigm for the entire humanity. Today, more than ever we need to commit toward an education that is not just about knowledge and skills for performance but also consciousness for an interconnected world and codependent existence that would benefit current and future generations. Academic programs and educational institutions that truly recognize the global responsibility that we have for a sustainable future need to do more than "green-wash" their educational business as usual. It requires us to transform our strategic priorities toward new approaches that center around shared values and common good responsibilities. It demands us to question education and see its contribution toward career developments and knowledge creation. It requires us to embrace science with a renewed sense of wonder, devotion and discovery centered around deeper and more spiritually centered leadership consciousness.

Marco's Views: I, Marco, have done a similar journey to Alfredo and have learned to question and review my western, Italian and

Catholic value systems and challenge them by encountering people in marginal societal situations and by learning from indigenous worldviews all over the world. These transformational journeys are important for everyone, no matter the different paths they may take or the diverse traditions and values systems they originate from. The sustainability leadership paradigm would obviously require the disposition of the leader to be open to change and be changed. In other words, these personal encounters with diversity (the I and thou) are essential transformational journeys that mold the leader's disposition and sensitivity toward global socio-diversity, natural biodiversity, and politico-economic institutional and organizational diversities. The ultimate meaning of these diversity encounters is to prepare each one of us to respond to our leadership call as catalysts for transformational, agents of change, or disruptors of the status quo. No matter the different leadership call we have at different times and in different contexts, these pre-dispositions are essential for making our role centered around the common good and rooted on our sensitive capacity to perceive the interconnectedness of sustainability as human and sentient beings.

CHAPTER V:

DOES ONE SIZE FIT ALL?

"No problem can be solved from the same level of consciousness that created it." —Albert Einstein

"We do not inherit the Earth from our ancestors; we borrow it from our children." —Native American Proverb

"Life's most persistent and urgent question is, 'What are you doing for others?'" —Martin Luther King Jr.

ONE SIZE FITS ALL LEADER?

It is essential to answer this question; otherwise, it will not be possible to lead or to establish the grounds for leadership within the path towards sustainable development. If there is only one universal prototype of leadership that may be applied everywhere, the situation would be very different from one which recognizes significant differences (attributes, factors and ingredients) according to the circumstances (economic model, sectors of the economy, type of corporation). To address this central question adequately, it demands going beyond today's simplified debate.

This book concludes that one size does not fit all; thus, that there are some "secret ingredients" contained in the development and formation of leaders and leadership that a good understanding of sustainable development demands.

Some complementary questions still remain to be addressed:

- *Will any good and successful leader, in the various areas of human activity (marketing, technological development), be also a good leader in the realm of sustainability?*
- *Will any good form of leadership be a good road towards sustainability leadership?*
- *Does sustainable development, as a paradigm of development and human transformation, shift and/or redefine "the core elements" of the new SL paradigm, and how does it do so?*

These are not rhetorical questions. To address these questions forces us to first have a clear and meaningful debate on what sustainable development is all about. We will address this later in the book.

For many decades, it has been said that "a manager is a manager", no matter which area of human activity she or he is involved. Many are extrapolating the same idea to the notion of a leader: "a leader is a leader no matter where leadership is being applied".

If this approach is accepted -the existence of a "universal" manager or leader-- then, we could state that good managers could easily and effectively be moved (transferred)from one activity (or sector) to the next, at a very low cost and without changes in the predicted outcomes. The various spaces of leadership are not an intervening variable. It all depends on the quality of the person involved and not on the context. This understanding means that one is implicitly advocating that 'management/leadership' and 'managers/leaders' operate (move, act-upon) on the same axis of performance. Let us call this "the universal axis of management/leadership".

If a leader is a leader no matter where, then, it also means that changes in the nature of activities -corporate, government, sustainability-do not change the core of a leader. For example, one could be a leader in an agricultural division, urban division, or industry division of a given organization and, in principle, always be an excellent leader. To address the impacts of leadership as the intervening variable, one would need to move just over the same axis of leadership values, attributes and performance. This means that there is no need for a change in paradigm, because there is no need or requirement at all to change the agreed core values, core vision, etc.

- *Is this possible?*
- *Is this true?*
- *Is this desirable?*
- *Is this the same for all leaders?*
- *Is this true for managers but not for leaders?*
- *Is this true for leaders and not managers?*

Contrary to the view that One-Size-Fits-All, and contrary to the existence of a paradigm where there is one-universal-axis-of-management/leadership, our experience demonstrates that this hypothesis is not necessarily true, or even possible. In the end, if we say that SL is a different paradigm of leadership, all together, because of the nature of sustainable development, one is implicitly postulating that each activity, or situation, possesses, demands, and requires its own (different) axis (core) of management/leadership.

The above has been proven in politics: a good corporate leader is not necessarily a good president. The same is true of hospitals: a good doctor may not be a good leader or managing director. Therefore, we state that it is imperative to recognize what is called here "the multiple axes of management/leadership'. This means that notions of leaders' attributes, leadership effectiveness and performance and standards of delivery and evaluation are quite different in different activities. Therefore, the axis of management/leadership shifts when one moves from one activity to another.

Let me share some personal experience here. For many years, in the institution I (Alfredo) used to work with, it was believed that they had to promote good performing technical people to the position of management/leadership within their respective areas. A shift with no change in the content. Thus, a good urban economist, or a good urban architect, would be promoted to become chief of the urban department or urban development division. This situation was replicated in almost all sectors of the economy (e.g., in agriculture an agronomist, in industries an industrial engineer, in human resource development a social psychologist).

In this case, the majority of performance indicators were mostly technical in nature. At that time, it was very rare to find that the institution brought someone from another sector. The management/leadership model was based on the respective technical and/or professional expertise. This is a typical example of a one axis management/leadership model. In hindsight, were they good managers/leaders? A few were good, but the large majority were not.

This is not something that happened, or happens, only in my former institution. It also happens everywhere today. A good example that illustrates the situation, is the debate we observe today as to whether an organization should be managed/led by a technical expertise on what that organization does. Should, could, they?

The same happens in the realm of politics: as stated earlier, whether a good private corporate manager, or corporate owner, would be a good senator, mayor, or president. Perhaps, in this situation the debate should be different as we are talking about a collective public good. But, at least two questions are relevant to address:

- *Is it the same to be a leader or manager of a private good than it is a public good?*
- *Is it the same to lead or manage a corporation than it is to lead or manage a country?*

When I was in a prestigious US university, we were taught that there was no difference in paradigm as regards to managing an international development institution or managing a McDonalds. As a student, we spent lots of time digging into such propositions. In some practical areas, it looks like this way of defining the paradigm of management is true. However, I refer to these practical areas as areas geared to improving the management functions. This is not the real core of such (development) institutions.

THE DIFFERENT AXIS OF LEADERSHIP

Thus, if the answer to the first question was 'no' (i.e., that they are different), then, we must be open to seriously consider a different paradigm of management and leadership. In particular, one would affirm that a leader in the field of sustainability is understood to operate in a different axis of leadership compared to any other leader belonging to another sector of society (corporate sector). This understanding has tremendous implications for the debate we are having today on SL. It follows that one is stating we are talking about a completely different creature.

So, how do we bring together the universal aspects of leadership or management with those that are considered unique? To be able to address this question, the situation we are against must be understood as having two layers of attributes of leaders:

One layer, which contains the attributes that may be conceived as universal to any leader (engaged, resilient, effective, compassionate...) to improve the existing management functions and,

Another layer, which must contain the rather unique attributes of a leader in the field of sustainability. It is these two layers of attributes that define the proposed two axes management approach to evaluation and performance.

Layers of Conscious Sustainability Leadership

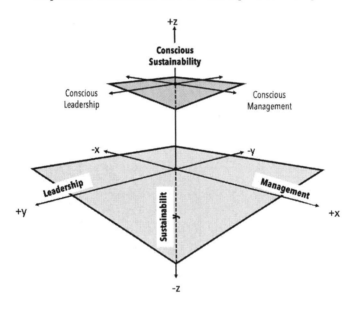

Figure 5: The axes and layers for conscious sustainability leadership and management

Continuing with my institutional experience, I found years later that my institution changed its approach of one axis management/leadership. It adopted a framework that responded to the universality of management attributes. Thus, a good manager was a good manager, no matter where they were located inside the institution. It was all beyond technical knowledge. This often happens when an institution grows too fast and bureaucratizes everything. As the pendulum swung, it was advocated that such specific technical knowledge, or otherwise, was easy to acquire. This is to me an implementation of "the theory of a single axis to management and leadership". Here, the nature defined within this approach becomes the all-around sufficient condition for a good management and a good leader.

I do not think that the two approaches have not been reconciled yet.

During my later years, they created a new creature in management: the "integrators". Those who could be in a world dominated by a great deal of diversity, and found ways to unite them.

Is all the above applicable to leaders on sustainability and to SL? All of this must be clarified and nurtured.

One early conclusion here: we are facing an interesting dialectic situation. On the one hand, we claim the uniqueness of the attributes embodied in a sustainability leader, making this paradigm unique (i.e., multiple axes). But, on the other hand, these attributes are really unique only in relation to the singular nature of the area to be managed: sustainable development (with all its dimensions).

The attributes of a sustainability leader are born out of an understanding of that uniqueness. In this case, it is definitely the uniqueness of sustainable development that makes the leaders on sustainability unique.

In essence, there is no One-Size-Fits-All leader as we are to embrace and advocate "the theory of multiple axes to management and leadership".

CHAPTER VI:
THE PARADIGM SHIFT

"Human self-understanding changes with time, and so also human consciousness deepens." —**Pope Francis**

"Poetry is the lifeblood of rebellion, revolution, and the raising of consciousness." —**Alice Walker**

"Offend in neither word nor deed. Eat with moderation. Live in your heart. Seek the highest consciousness. Master yourself according to the law. This is the simple teaching of the awakened." —**The Buddha**

"The key to growth is the production of higher dimensions of consciousness into our awareness." —**Lao Tzu**

A compelling reason for addressing leadership once again is our deep feeling and practical experience that there is a major paradigm shift worldwide, including the fields of economics, politics, corporate, institutional, technology, governance, and social. The rules of the game have changed, and we see the manifestations in both developed and developing countries. A major accelerator of those shifts has been the power and effectiveness of social media, an example of which we see now daily as many marches and social movements act in a coordinated and simultaneous fashion all over the world. The movements of "Fridays for Future" and subsequent "Fire Drill Fridays" are a prime example on matters related to climate change.[21]

The above demands the creation of the necessary spaces and instances to address different paradigms of leadership in relationship to those shifts. In many respects, it seems evident that leadership has either not recognized such a shift, or it has major problems in adjusting to operate and guide a new future. This shift is affecting and modifying each and every aspect of human activity, including the nature and scope of leadership itself. Leadership must also evolve accordingly.

Let's focus only on four of those activities: environment, economics, citizenship, and human transformation.

ENVIRONMENTAL PERCEPTIONS

In the last half of a century, the debate on environment, ecology, nature and sustainability has dramatically changed. Perhaps, one may argue that these changes have not been sufficient, or that they have not really affected enough the content of the debate. However, it is certain that it has greatly influenced the level of public and collective awareness of the negative impacts of environmental destruction and natural resource depletion. Today, it is much more robust and prominent in the realm of different forms of communication.

Many people, academics, scientists and politicians have been sharing, with the rest of the public, the importance and the corresponding negative effects of, for example, global warming, the pollution of the oceans, and the depletion of biodiversity worldwide, and type of crises the world is, and may be, facing for more in the future. "The Tragedy of the Commons" of Garrett Hardin, "Silent Spring" of Rachel Carson, "Limits to Growth" of the Club of Rome, and "Our Common Future" Gro Brundtland, are some examples of voices we have heard for decades, but where the response was always meager. There are hundreds more examples.

The same has happened at the political level. Only recently, and for many reasons, several politicians have given priority to issues having to do with sustainable development. Perhaps, politicians cannot afford not to address these issues because of power redistribution, intergenerational justice, social costs embodied, interest groups demand, etc., in response to what is happening in our environment and ecology, at the country and global levels. With one or two exceptions, candidates for the highest office of a given country (e.g., Austria) have won elections with a 'green' political platform. The recent move towards globalization and neoliberal economics have delayed the ability of citizens to protect and conserve the environment.

Sustainability is now referred to within almost any website or different means of advertising. Whether those who promote such advertising are actually doing something worth accounting for it is a big question.

Economic Paradigm Shifts

There is no doubt that there has been a shift in the 'economic calculus' of traditional economics, and explain why. We will not address the many new economic paradigms that are coming up for serious consideration. It goes beyond the scope of this book to address Circular Economics, Justice Economics, Ecological Economics, Spiritual Economics, Love Economics, etc.

In the economic calculus, we have been accustomed to deal with the so-called "1st round-effects" from market transactions (its net direct benefits). The buying, selling, paying and receiving. Behind this 1st round-effect is the concept of efficiency, competitiveness, productivity, competition, willingness to pay, and so on.

The idea in focusing only on the 1st round-effects assumes that those transactions did not create significant positive or negative-external-effects on the rest of the economy. There is not a residual in need to be accounted for. Thus, the present approach holds that what happens during the 2nd or 3rd round-effects of those market transactions are to be considered almost irrelevant. Thus, traditional 'welfare economics' has mainly focused on what happens during the 1st round (e.g., costs and benefits); these are the costs and benefits that really count.

However, today, the greatest source of benefits and costs (particularly costs) are contained in the 2nd or 3rd round-effects. This includes the impacts on the environment, ecology, health, and sustainability.

Thus, for some time, any of us began to claim that the attention must be directed towards the nature, scope and amounts of the other round-effects. In essence, the fact that one recognizes the relative importance of the 2nd and 3rd round-effects is what gives a new foundation to a claim for a need of a new leadership paradigm, focusing specifically on sustainability. This is a major departure from traditional economics. The economics of only 1st round-effects.

Today, this reality facing economics and the economic analysis of decision making –the engagement into the net impacts of the 2nd and 3rd round-effects—demands to look for a type of leader, and a form of leadership, that is sensitive, aware, and responsive to this major change in the notion of human welfare with its causes and conditions. In particular, the claim here is that the net benefits accrued during the 1st round could be wiped out by the costs embodied in the 2nd and 3rd round-effects.

Economists began recognizing this reality a long time ago. "The Theory of Public Goods" is a relevant example, and most recently through the important "Theory of Externalities".

One of the most graphic presentations of the above theories is in the article The Tragedy of the Commons (Science, 1968) by Garrett Hardin. A must read.[22] The author describes the behavior of two shepherds in a prairie, where there was no previously recognized assignment of property rights. An apparent mechanism for exclusion. Thus, it was perceived as no one's land. Nowhere the shepherds had preassigned rules of engagement –rules of access, ownership, use, management and conservation. Thus, there was no clarity as regards to how many sheep each of the shepherds may bring into that prairie. Thus, it was a situation where the incentives were such that it was "rational" to bring as many sheep as possible. The story goes that, in the end, the prairie was completely destroyed by the two herds: the tragedy of the commons.

The above may be a rather simple story. But its policy prescription was not. To avoid the tragedy of the commons, Hardin's policy recommendation is to privatize the property right to the prairie! For him, the assignment of private property rights will ensure exclusion, and exclusion will preserve the prairie. The situation of the prairie and the policy prescription are still advocated today (e.g., creating national parks to preserve biodiversity).

Understanding the potential impacts that a lack of exclusion may have on the access of a given natural resource heightens the importance of inter-spatial (through space) and inter-temporal (through time) effects of economic and social activities. The paradigm shift shows us, for example, that the boundaries of a given corporation are not just those walls around the factory; these boundaries are as far as pollution goes. This also applies to a large number of issues and situations, like global warming, ozone layer depletion, ocean pollution...etc.

In addition, this demonstrates that the short-term impacts of human activities are not all the economic calculus must consider. It must also focus on long-term effects (e.g., climate).

All of these shifts do change the way we are to make private and public choices, and change the approach we are to use in order to adopt and to evaluate the goodness of those choices.

Equally important in this paradigm shift is to seriously consider the relevance of the design and implementation of economic, social, institutional and political 'incentives', to avoid those negative external effects described above. One must consider both the market and the non-market incentives.   These are incentives that are geared to modify both political and corporate management decisions.

These are incentives that need to be felt within a particular sector as well as across sectors of economic activity. These are incentives that should modify country behaviors at the global levels. Thus, the importance of understanding the nature of our interdependence and the priority we must give to interdisciplinary work.

Part of the shift in incentives structures towards sustainable development must be accelerated and consolidated with what I call "environmental macroeconomics" (e.g., pricing policies, fiscal policies, and trade policies). As of today, we lack an environmental macroeconomic analyst, and universities must do something about it.

THE COLLECTIVE POWER OF CITIZENSHIP

In the past, most leadership paradigms and the figure of the leader was "top down". The notion of the 'one leader for all people'. This is not any longer the case. Different strata of the population are now expressing different forms of leadership worldwide; e.g., the Arab

Spring, the Occupy Movement, Friday for Futures, the U.N. Social Summit for Climate Change. These are all forms of co-leadership.

Also, as an intergenerational phenomenon, the younger generations and their many leaders have shattered the glass ceiling! They are expressing leadership in many different ways, including community leadership, youth council leadership, and collective co-leadership in general. Here, decisions do not come from a cupula of a few persons. Leadership is constructed by all of those involved.

Today, due to population, demography, urbanization, biodiversity depletion, pollution of the oceans, destruction of natural forests, killing of animals, rapid depletion of the genetic pool, water and air pollution, natural disasters...awareness has increased almost everywhere. Technology has contributed to an increased awareness of the general public, especially via communication technologies and the spread of social media; so much so, that, today, we can instantaneously convoke worldwide actions and street rallies via the internet or via cellular phones.

The relative importance of citizens has exploded in relation to traditional governments and pyramidal institutions. This is particularly important in sustainable development and empowered citizenship, where both sustainability and empowerment go together. A major departure from the past.

This collective construct deviates immensely from the traditional leadership paradigms and the attributes of leaders. Contrary to these paradigms, what matters today is not the attribute of leaders but the collective attributes and emotions of citizens' movements. It is not just trust, but collective trust. It is not just emotions, but collective emotions.

The citizens' revolution of the 21st Century demands leaders that have this dual embodiment of leadership: individual and collective. A major change and breakthrough from the past.

HUMAN TRANSFORMATION: THE INNER AND OUTER SHIFTS

As for the abovementioned paradigm shift -individual and collective—there is yet another profound change and global trend we should recognize explicitly: inner and outer ecology of human transformation. This is the space for the recognition of human consciousness and the inner soul of leaders and leadership. This shift demands to recognize how leadership intensifies a given experience and the expansion of that experience. Today, the real challenge for a leader is not necessarily to have a very large portfolio of attributes (more is not necessarily better). The challenge is to deepen into a few, and self-realize them. One has to go far beyond a statement of facts, like the leader must be 'committed', 'patient' and compassionate. It is not just a slogan to characterize a given leader.

The real horizon is to self-realize 'patience', 'commitment' and 'compassion', understanding that these are not words, or things, but three states of being (among many). All attributes of leaders are states of being and as such they must be self-realized. These attributes are not things to have, or to possess, but these are states of the leader's inner-reality, which they have to be and to become.

In particular, this aspect of the paradigm shift we observe today demands that a leader must first embody compassion, and not just to know some sort of compassion. But, second, a leader must commit to the creation of a compassionate society (corporation). This is the collective expression of that attribute. It is here when the notion of individual and collective consciousness of leaders begins to make real sense. The characterization of the attributes of leaders is not only about an awareness creation process (though relevant), but, in the end, it is about a very subtle and deeper level of realization.

This new paradigm shift creates the necessary conditions so that leaders become self-realized beings on those attributes they are to bring into leadership. It is here when the notion of a "conscious leader" and "conscious leadership" begin to make sense.

In the academic context, and in the realm of university programs on leaders for sustainability, the new paradigm shift calls for two types of learning. One, called "vertical learning" (to be and to become: the being) –i.e., to acquire the type of knowledge that comes from within and to strengthen your inner self. Two, called "horizontal learning" (to know, to have and to do: the doing)—i.e., that form of knowledge which comes from our external environment and experience (activities designed to create awareness), as most traditional education programs are offering today.

The latter form of learning may be in the classroom or as a result of some environmental activities (cleaning a beach). The former form of learning will come out of a clear spiritual path of meditation, contemplation, yoga, prayer, productive silence, and much more. While these may be complementary, they are not necessarily the same. This is a theme that needs further development, but will not be treated explicitly here.

CHAPTER VII:
SUSTAINABLE DEVELOPMENT

"Sustainable development is development that meets the needs of the present without compromising the ability of future generations to meet their own needs." —Gro Harlem Brundtland

"Climate change is the greatest threat to human rights in the 21st century." —Mary Robinson

"Ours can be the first generation to end poverty – and the last generation to address climate change before it is too late." —Ban Ki-Moon

"To truly shift the needle, however, we need a new wave of triple bottom line (TBL) innovation and deployment. [...] Indeed, none of these sustainability frameworks will be enough, as long as they lack the suitable pace and scale - the necessary radical intent - needed to stop us all overshooting our planetary boundaries." —John Elkington

As stated before, the unique nature of the new paradigm of leadership proposed here is determined by our understanding of sustainable development. Thus, the uniqueness of a sustainable leader depends on how one understands the nature and scope of sustainable development. This chapter focuses on a very limited number of issues regarding sustainable development and its relationship to a new form of leadership.

Here, we focus on some definitions of sustainable development that clearly illustrate the linkages between sustainable development and the formation of leaders, and the construction of a new leadership paradigm.

THE TRIPLE BOTTOM LINE

There is no doubt that one of the most popular definitions of sustainable development is that of the 'triple bottom line': "for development to be sustainable it has to be economically sustainable, ecologically sustainable, and socially sustainable". This definition led to the 'sustainability triangle'.

The reason to bring this definition here is not its functionality but its comprehensiveness: economics, environment, and social. However, in practice, it is economics that has dominated the decision-making processes everywhere. This is to say that, in decision making and evaluation, the "economic calculus" has been primordial, and primus-inter-pares as regards the other two calculus, which have been residuals. As a result, it became necessary to create The Environmental Impact Statement (EIS) and The Social Impact Statement (SIS), to save a given investment from damaging the environment. Often, decision makers use these two impact statements as pro-forma, and the economic calculus being the essence of decisions.

Lots of debates have taken place over the last decades about the relationship between economics and the social dimensions of sustainability, and between economics and the environmental dimensions of sustainability. One is not suggesting here that the issues arising from those interactions have been settled. Far from it.

Each of those two interactions is pointing to a special kind of leader for sustainability.

Spheres of Sustainable Development

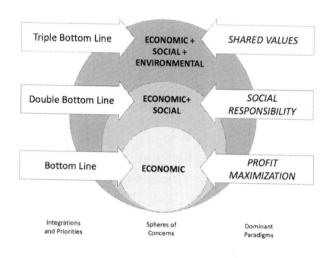

Figure 6: Integrated Spheres of Sustainable Development

However, here, we believe it is important to acknowledge the crucial connection that exists between the social dimension and the ecological dimension of sustainability. This is fundamental in addressing leadership within the context of sustainability and in the formation of leaders. This is the sustainability axis that most directly focuses on how the 'human factor' affects and shapes the relationship between human beings and nature.

The connection is strong and very rich. In fact, many academics and advocates have devoted their professional lives to establish the fact that the ecological crises we live on the planet today is always a social crisis. These are two interdependent phenomena. If one pays attention to the political dimensions of sustainability, attention to the axis of social and environment enables us to put a 'face' or a 'community' on the ecological crisis.

This definition of the triple bottom line is functional, but it is too simplistic in describing what sustainable development is all about. Two questions worth addressing:

- *How may this framework contribute to the construction of a new leadership paradigm?*
- *How does this framework contribute to identify some relevant attributes of a sustainability leader?*

Perhaps the merits of this definition are to open up a debate to a more multi-sectoral view of development, whereby the objective function to be optimized goes far beyond the maximization of profits (at the corporate level) and the maximization of national income (at the macro level). This means that sustainability is not just about maximizing Gross National Product (GNP), or some material expression of that.

However, this definition of sustainability heightens the importance of relevant trade-offs between three spheres:

- *i) economics and environment (green-capitalism),*
- *ii) economics and social (social-capitalism), and*
- *iii) environment and social (eco-socialism).*

The three sides of the sustainability triangle correspond to a very different political ideology and, thus, its importance to the debate on leadership.

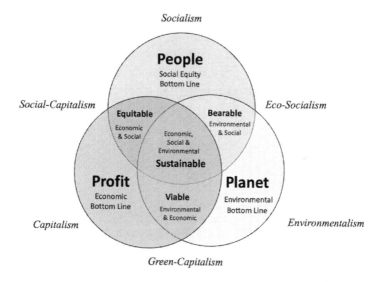

Sustainable Development as Integrated Bottom Lines
(Elkington Definition)

Figure 7: The Triple Bottom Line (TBL or 3BL) Definition

Since a lot has been said to date about social-capitalism and green-capitalism, we will pay some attention to the third proposition: "eco-socialism". For the time being, to me, the most important side of the triangle and ideology is "eco-socialism". Eco-Socialism was not born into a political party, including any socialist parties. This view arose in 2009, within the so-called World Social Forum, in Belem do Para, Brazil.[23] There was an International "Eco-Socialist Manifesto" which was written mainly by two people: John Bellamy Ester, an ecological Marxist, and Terisa Turner, an eco-feminist. At the meeting, and in her writings, she separates herself from two ideologies: conformist ecology with market proposals (green-capitalism) and the real socialism of Russia and China, where she sees that they possess an "anti-ecological productivism".

Eco-socialism proposes a reorganization of the production and consumption patterns we see today. Not only is there a concern for the change in productive relations and property relations, but for the entire structure of the productive apparatus. It is made clear that the market does not resolve, and that the impacts of origin and incidence (who pollutes and who is affected by pollution) are asymmetric at the expense of the poorest (social crisis). This calls for adopting a long-term approach with a great emphasis on the collective and the common good. All demand for a new role of leadership to implement a new industrial revolution. Finally, this vision changes the parameters that define a leader and a series of concepts such a leader will confront: welfare, development, competitiveness, sustainability, which implies leaving the capitalist way of solving the environmental problems.

Eco-socialism is an ideology (a paradigm) in itself. It represents an important line of thought and values that responds to a change in the reading of the current environmental crisis. One of the most important aspects of eco-socialism is to understand that the ecological crisis goes hand in hand with the social crisis, as two sides of the same coin. The poor live in ecologically poor environments. Otherwise they would be rich. Two interconnected crises. Crises that result from the same structural problems confronting our society. Today, the dominant criteria for leadership are those of productivity, profit, competitiveness ... of constant expansion. They result in the depletion and waste of our natural resources and the destabilization of existing ecological niches. The social crisis is exacerbated by the same causes; accelerated by globalization. Today we see that economies are globalized, but societies are not globalized.

In ecological terms, if there is to be a future worth living, the current economic system is deeply unsustainable and must be fundamentally changed and even better, replaced. Who is to lead this process, and how would one define that form of leadership? In essence, they advocate for a leader who will realize that deeper changes are required to create a new economic and social system, where the dimensions are not only quantitative but qualitative: lifestyles, different forms of well-being ... The leader will have to move societies and productive systems from the extractive and the exploitation, to the conservation of resources and to find completely different forms of economic growth and job creation.

Therefore, it is important to retain the following elements: the importance of the trade-offs between social and ecological capital and sustainability, the set of values that support the debates within that relationship, and the political ideology that accompanies both ends of that side of sustainable development.

BRUDTLAND'S DEFINITION

This definition was widely known after the book "Our Common Future" (1987) by Gro Harlem Brundtland, former Prime Minister of Norway, and former Director General of the World Health Organization. For her, sustainability was directly related to the capacity of this generation to satisfy its needs, while not constraining future generations to satisfy their needs.

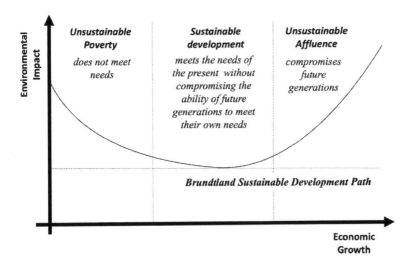

Figure 8: The Brundtland Sustainable Development Definition

This definition brought several important dimensions and attributes for the nurturing of a leadership paradigm. In particular,

The recognition of future generations

That future generations have rights, like the right to life, the right to a clean and safe environment, and the right to healthy foods. This is not just a matter of philanthropy or hands outs. It is a matter of rights and responsibilities, as it demands policies, investments programs and projects, financial resources and projects. Our preoccupation for future generations is also a matter of morals and ethics; with ethics and morals as attributes of the new leader. It also opens a debate to 'what constitutes a future generation?' Are they already here on the planet? Is this just a matter of age differences or there is some other way to understand present and future generations?

The importance of the long-term

Most countries and leaders are very short-term oriented. Leaders have to embody a capacity to not only accept a longer-term but to create the ability to construct it! This requires a different way of thinking because the long-term is not a linear summation of the short terms. The leader will necessitate to wear a pair of lenses and adopt an approach to what we, as a society, will have to do now and in the medium-term. To be a leader on sustainable development requires a very good understanding of the long-term.

The explicit yardstick of 'human needs'

Here is when the definition begins to decay. How a given society defines those needs. Which needs? The needs of people in developed countries, or in developing countries? These questions are particularly important when we come to the realization that our planet is finite (e.g., material balance). For developing countries, those material needs may be equivalent to half or one third of those in developed countries, in terms of the potential and actual use of natural resources and of those services from the environment (clean air). This is a very controversial issue. What is a need? Is everything we desire/want a need? In societies driven by consumption at any cost, this is not a trivial debate. This is why new leaders for sustainability will come face to face with "conscious consumption" and establish the grounds for the adequate preservation of this planet.

The concept of 'satisfaction'

This is something very subjective and, thus, very much culturally based and determined. Is it satisfaction about consumption and the satisfaction of material necessities, or is it about happiness? The answer is not trivial, but it is at the center stage of sustainable leadership. The definition of satisfaction would have been extremely different if instead of satisfying needs, different generations would endure happiness and joy.

As we will see in a moment, these attributes of the Brundtland definition will have a tremendous influence on the way one defines leadership, leadership for sustainability, and the new paradigm.

SFEIR-YOUNIS' DEFINITION

Almost during the same period of time, I engaged in a major study of sustainability at the level of projects and programs in developing countries, financed by the World Bank. This was an ex-post evaluation study, based on audit and evaluation reports of a very large number of completed operations. The research found plenty of material regarding sustainability in about 625 completed operations (projects). A 'revealed preference approach' was used to classify and codify the data and information about sustainability.

This empirical study concluded that "sustainability was an ability to attain a balance among all forms of capital participating in the development process". The study recognized at least the following forms of capital and their interactions: physical capital (e.g., infrastructure, buildings), financial capital (e.g., money, financial instruments), human capital (e.g., intelligence, knowledge, skills), natural capital (e.g., environment and ecology), institutional capital (e.g., organizations, human rights, and incentives), cultural capital (e.g., customs, habits, dance, music) and, later on, I added spiritual capital (e.g., human inner self, ethics).

Several aspects of this definition are important in constructing a new sustainability leadership paradigm.

The notion of capital was widely expanded. It opened up and disaggregated the first definition of sustainability: "the sustainability triangle". As such, it illustrated better the notions of social capital and man-made capital. Thus, several of the issues raised earlier apply here.

The recognition that the interactive parameters between those forms of capital and the attainment of sustainable development were not zero, as assumed in the past. The trade-offs and the different forms of interdependence among various forms of capital was expanded and improved. Thus, it was not only the relationship of man-made capital (physical and financial capital) with natural capital (the only influencer), but with many other forms of capital. These multiple interactions will determine the level and composition of sustainable development. The attention must be paid to ALL those forms of capital—the influence on natural capital and to sustainable development.

The way it illustrated how to attain the balance across sectors of the economy was completely different (e.g., education, health, public works, agriculture, fisheries). For example, the study found that in order to attain sustainable development within the infrastructure sector, investments had to be more physical and financial capital intensive. While in the case of a rural development program, the attaining of development sustainability was more natural and human capital intensive.

Sustainable Development as Integrated Capitals
(Sfeir-Younis Definition)

Figure 9: The Sfeir-Younis Definition of Sustainability

This approach was also used to lead in the determination of the true nature of poverty, and how to get people out of absolute poverty. What was found there was that the key ingredient was institutional capital, and within that capital, it was ownership and human rights. Furthermore, this paradigm was also applied onto two longitudinal studies, during a 25-30 year-period, to evaluate the impacts of foreign development assistance in Bolivia and Nepal. In essence, those two country studies revealed quite clearly the practical decisions of leaders within those societies, and the outcomes of a leadership paradigm. These studies showed the lack of leaders for sustainability in the course of making overall development decisions, which would ensure proper sustainable development outcomes. The economic paradigm of the time dominated the leadership.

CHAPTER VIII:
THE PROFOUNDNESS OF SUSTAINABLE DEVELOPMENT

"What we are doing to the forests of the world is but a mirror reflection of what we are doing to ourselves and to one another."–**Mahatma Gandhi**

"We lack leadership capable of striking out on new paths and meeting the needs of the present with concern for all and without prejudice towards coming generations. The establishment of a legal framework which can set clear boundaries and ensure the protection of ecosystems has become indispensable; otherwise, the new power structures based on the techno-economic paradigm may overwhelm not only our politics but also freedom and justice." –**Pope Francis**

"Meditation is the dissolution of thoughts in Eternal awareness or Pure consciousness without objectification, knowing without thinking, merging finitude in infinity." –**Voltaire**

The connection between sustainable development and leadership is a very profound and engaging one. To understand what is at stake, we have to leave those definitions aside for a moment –e.g., we need to move away from the trees and look at the whole forest. Today, it is important to distinguish the different 'visions' that exist about sustainable development. There are several of these visions, each of which having a tremendous influence on how one is to construct a new paradigm for leadership in sustainable development. The following visions are worth considering.

1. Sustainable Development as corresponding to one specific stage of development

Specifically, most people accept that there are stages and these usually are: (i) economic growth, (ii) socio economic development, and (iii) sustainable development. They are neither separate nor inclusive of each other.

Economic growth addresses the processes of capital accumulation (i.e., how much, how fast an economy accumulates capital). This is associated with investments of all sorts in the different forms of capital addressed earlier (e.g., physical, financial, human). If one is to make a cartoon out of this, economic growth has to do with how much and how fast the 'cake' grows.

Socio-economic development has born out of a concern with equity and justice. It has to do with 'who' benefits from development and growth. We could say that it focuses on who eats the cake. Thus, a great deal of debate about wealth creation, poverty, and income distribution.

Sustainable development, which was defined earlier, focuses not on how fast the cake grows, or on who eats the cake, but on "how long' will the cake last, because most natural resources --and the environmental services of those resources-- are exhaustible.

Sustainable Stages of Development
The Cake Analogy

Economic Concerns
How fast does the cake grow?
Development as growth

Social Concerns
Who eats the cake?
Development as rights

Environmental Concerns
How long will the cake last?
Development as sustainability

Figure 10: Sustainable Development Stages – Cake Analogy

However, I have stated many times that these stages and the different forms of development engaged in them, do not end with sustainable development. The ultimate form of development is "Conscious Development". I have also called this "Empowered Development". It is a must to bring into the debate on leadership conscious production, conscious consumption, conscious trade and marketing, and conscious human transformation. In terms of how the other stages were presented, we could say that Conscious Development focuses on 'what' are the ingredients of the cake (i.e., in terms of quantity and quality. For a true leader, conscious means to be empowered to set the right vision and make the right choices, it means to be empowered itself, individually, as well as to empower the collective, it means to bring together all forms of outer power and inner power together, and it means to show clearly the critical path to self-realize that state of empowerment. This is particularly relevant to citizen leadership. These elements will be taken up again when presenting the new paradigm: "Conscious Sustainability Leadership".

The aspects presented above are vital when it comes to defining attributes of leaders for sustainability, and to improving the existing paradigm of leadership.

2. SUSTAINABLE DEVELOPMENT AS A COLLECTION OF VALUES

The outcomes we see today are the results of choices and decisions we make, individually or collectively. But the decisions we make are essentially determined by our values and beliefs system. Thus, the values we hold dear to ourselves will set the boundaries regarding how we see and define sustainability. There is a direct correlation between values and sustainable development (e.g., choices regarding our long-term future). Today, traditional development is hostage to materialistic and individualistic values. Examples of these values are competition, hoarding, greed, exclusion, profits, etc. These are values heavily dominated by an individual and a social ego. This is often called the neoliberal economic and social system. A system that has led to the very rapid depletion of all-natural resources. A value system where "more is always better"; i.e., one needs to accumulate all the time.

Contrary to this value system, sustainable development is to be attained responsibly, society must nurture with collective values. Sustainable development is clearly a collective concern. It is not an "I", it is a "We". Examples of these collective values are: interdependence, cooperation, solidarity, collective rights, responsibility, caring, sharing, love, compassion, and more. These values are not just words. These are not just attributes of a healthy road towards sustainability. These values are states of being and, as such, these values must be self-realized. This means that the new leader must embody these values, and not just advocate those values.

The leader must become interdependent. It means that the leader must create the space and the conditions so everyone in society self-realizes these collective values.

This is a very different paradigm than the one advocated by most universities which have developed programs on sustainability leadership. This is a program of self-realization.

We cannot allow that all the categories of analysis, leaders, leadership, sustainability, development, values, etc., are 'things'. That all is just knowledge and not wisdom. That all is scientific and not intuitive. Mahatma Gandhi said that we will only take care (conserve) what we love. Not what it has the highest market price. Love is not a thing. Similarly, without cooperation and solidarity –two fundamental collective values of sustainability-- we will never be able to attain such sustainability. All these values must be ingrained within the leadership paradigm and be a key attribute of leaders on sustainability.

Let me repeat, these values are not just words. These are inner states of human reality and, as such, we have to self-realize them. Leadership is a road to self-realization at the individual and collective levels; it is not trivial. This is why we pay lots of attention to the importance of spirituality.

3. SUSTAINABLE DEVELOPMENT AS A BUNDLE OF RIGHTS

Many people see development as a collection of rights: "The Universal Declaration of Human Rights (UDHR)", "Civil and Political Right (CPR)", "Economic, Social and Cultural Rights (ESCR)", and "The Right to Development (TRD)". These rights have constructed the foundation of the so-called "Right Based Approach to Development (RBAD)",[24] where there is this notion that there are certain goods and services --including environmental and ecological ones-- are subject to rights (assignment of rights, human rights valuation), and not necessarily subject to market valuation. Some examples are: health, education, air, water, biodiversity, ozone layer, climate, oceans, glaciers, security, stability, peace, and many others, under the category of public goods, nationally and globally.

When addressing sustainable development, it is essential to note the bundle of rights that accompanies it. It is not just about human rights but also the right to development (i.e., a country cannot limit the right to development of another country). The bundle of rights linked to sustainability is a derived form of rights: the right to life and the right to a safe and clean environment. These have given rise to ecological rights, environmental rights, the rights of future generations and the right to nature.

This view has opened the gate to important debates as to whether the 'market' should dominate decisions about sustainability, or should we promote a society that is mainly governed by rights, as suggested by the RBAD. A person, a community, a region or a country has the right to develop, it has the right to the path towards sustainable development. No person, community, or country has the right to limit that path towards sustainability.

This is a fundamental issue because it confronts heads-on the neoliberal system, which predominates in the world today. For example, this neoliberal system has resulted in excessive pollution, global warming, biodiversity depletion, elimination of animal and plant species, etc.

The impacts of violating the above-mentioned rights are asymmetric as, for example, Small Island States may have to bear huge costs from global warming, compared to the costs of those who are the principal CO_2 polluters. This pollution may become a significant constraint to the development of someone else.

A society governed by rights and not the market has a very different approach to institutions, incentives, governance, etc. A classic example is that of education as a human right and not as a commodity. This paradigm may be applied to all goods that humanity possesses in common.

All of the above have lots of diverse ramifications into the alternative definition of leadership, and into the identification of the relevant attributes of leaders in this millennium.

4. Sustainable Development as a 'Style of Life'

Most countries are imitating the 'style of life' of the so-called developed countries. And all the conceptual framework and social grammar go into that direction. The style of life comes from the definitions embraced in such areas as human welfare, socio-economic development, transformation, economic and social institutions, competitiveness, value and worth, etc. This demands a constantly increasing production and consumption, expanding the scale of activities, with the corresponding impacts on natural resource depletion and the deterioration of the environment. This is perhaps the most important challenge facing leaders today, as it demands a major shift in paradigm. Leaders will have to define and project not only their own style of life but they will have to move societies towards adopting a style of life which will be compatible with an acceptable sustainable future in this planet. We all know that today's lifestyle (material life) is totally unsustainable. Thus, the key question is to define how will leaders provoke the needed change so that we have a future?

To propose changes in the present lifestyle is a politically controversial issue, as many people in developed countries are neither willing nor prepared to sacrifice their lifestyle for the benefit of the whole humanity. No doubt that this position is fed by the ego, greed, and unacceptable collective behavior. Perhaps, more complex than this behavior is the demand that people in developing countries are exercising to have the same style of life than those of developed countries. Some leaders are saying that such a situation is inevitable as production and consumption is dominated by the corporate world within developed countries; and for these countries to grow (so they say), they must find markets in developing countries. This approach is an "accelerator" to the rapid destruction of our planet. This theme must not be outside the domain of a paradigm on leadership for sustainability.

5. SUSTAINABLE DEVELOPMENT AS A POWER STRUCTURE

Behind any model of natural resources management there is a power structure. The power comes from the ownership, access and use of a given natural resource, as property rights (private or common property rights) lead to a different form of sustainable development. An illustration is the case of water as a natural resource. In many neoliberal economies, the public authority and parliaments have enabled the assignment of private rights over water.

Private rights create a very different form of sustainability because of the implied incentives, valuation, productivity (over space and time, etc.) than that of a system of public rights or rights in trust whereby the government is either the owner or the guarantor of those rights. Different property rights regimes lead to different means, instruments, and critical paths towards the aim of sustainable development objectives.

One cannot de-link sustainability from power structures.

6. SUSTAINABLE DEVELOPMENT AS A STATE OF HUMAN CONSCIOUSNESS

If a new vision has to emerge in the world today, it is evident that such a vision will have to come about as an outcome of a new and higher level of human consciousness (individual and collective consciousness). It is this new consciousness that will open the space for a new vision. The old consciousness does not have the content and attributes to lead us towards sustainable development. As property rights create power structures, collective values, which we have to self-realize, individually or collectively, play a crucial role in the relationship between human consciousness and sustainability.

The above forces us to see sustainable leaders as highly conscious individuals, having a "wide-lens-view" of reality, and as having the capacity to contain (store, embrace) the true reality we face today in this planet. Here, we are talking about being conscious of other human beings, conscious of sentient beings, conscious of nature and Natural Law, and conscious of themselves.

It will be this new and expanded consciousness, for example, that will enable each of us to understand the Earth as a being, and not just as a thing. For the moment, most people see the Earth as a collection of material things to be consumed or to be disposed of, and these foreclose infinite options for a better future. The attention of sustainability is not only with human beings, but with all sentient beings and nature.

As a result of a new consciousness, this stage of sustainable development leads towards the empowerment of people. The empowerment of citizens. Conscious Development is also "empowered development"; both, the inner and the outer empowerment of people.

The empowerment of people as a paradigm will greatly change the definition of a leader, and the foundations of leadership. This is the essence of sustainability that makes possible a conscious sustainable leadership paradigm, where individual human consciousness and social consciousness are an integral part of social capital (see the triangle of sustainability).

Consciousness for Sustainable Development

Sustainable Development as Realization

Transcendence Level
Need for conscious leadership as self-actualization and self-awareness for universal well-being.

Freedom from Ignorance

Sustainable Development as Freedom

Development Level
Need for sustainable development as better life conditions for people, planet, prosperity, peace and partnerships.

Freedom from Poverty

Freedom From Death

Sustainable Development as Right

Survival Level
Need for human rights and security gaining access to safety, food, shelter, air, water, work dignity, social equity, gender equality, health, education, and belonging.

Figure 11: The Pyramid of Conscious Sustainability Leadership

This is a radical departure from the existing leadership paradigms.

In particular, to avoid the many negative effects of economic growth and capital accumulation, we have to expand and deepen our human and social consciousness. Thus, in many ways, the paradigm proposed here suggests the opposite critical path towards a better world and to the healing of the planet. First conscious and empowered development and then the rest. It will be as a result of human consciousness that we will be able to establish the true goals of economic growth, quality of life, and human welfare. More material wealth is not a sufficient condition to live a better life. We all know that.

And, to attain the above, we do not need to sacrifice our quality of life, our identity, our sense of belonging, our inner peace, or our collective peace.

The new leadership paradigm which emerges from the above will result in radical changes of several concepts and definitions like welfare, development, rights and responsibilities, etc.

A new form of leadership must have the consciousness to avoid market failures, inter-temporal and spatial externalities, wrong systems of valuation, inadequate assignment of property rights, weak forms of governance, the irreversibility in resource use, destroy our global public goods, etc.

CHAPTER IX:
THE ETHICS OF SUSTAINABILITY

*"Non-violence leads to the highest ethics, which is the goal of all evolution. Until we stop harming all other living beings, we are still savages." —**Thomas A. Edison***

*"People who are truly strong lift others up. People who are truly powerful bring others together." —**Michelle Obama***

*"Let me give you a definition of ethics: It is good to maintain and further life, it is bad to damage and destroy life." —**Albert Schweitzer***

*"The more clearly we can focus our attention on the wonders and realities of the universe about us, the less taste we shall have for destruction." — **Rachel Carson***

In the last chapters, it was shown where the frontier of development lies and, thus, where we should move the paradigm of leadership.

On that frontier, which is determined by the level of human consciousness, we also have to take into account the issues of ethics and morals. Considerations of ethics will enable leaders to change or revert the critical path of development and human transformation. It is in this context of ethics and morals that a true leader establishes the grounds to pass from 'what it is' to 'what it should be'. It is at the level of the collective where this unique leader will be able to create a citizen's ethic-culture (or a corporate's ethics-culture) which, in turn, will bring to the fore a series of issues that are often forgotten by other leaders (see below).

The same applies to governance of the global commons. As we observe today, it is undesirable that the governance of global public goods, for example, is often exercised within an ethical and moral vacuum. We would expect that a truly conscious leader will support a path towards "ethical governance".

This is relevant as leaders have to define the "objective function" of leadership and, thus, define the optimal ways society has to allocate and conserve all forms of available capital, which participates in the development process. In other words, we cannot have leaders that allow the practice of economics and politics also within an ethical and moral vacuum.

To illustrate this, let as list some of the areas and issues that have the greatest ethical connotations in sustainable development:

The importance to commit everyone to a 'life manifesto' (all forms of life).

Decision making has many distinctive impacts. Thus, in measuring or valuing the potential impacts of the leaders' actions, one must take into consideration the impacts on all human beings, all sentient beings and nature. Then, the essence of this manifesto of life is not an anthropocentric view of sustainability and conscious development. The conscious leader must embrace all forms of life that exist on the planet and all must be considered.

The genuine concern for all future generations.

As expressed in Brundtland's definition of sustainable development, societies must take into account all future generations. It is central to pass-on to them a 'healed planet', with a composition of ecological and environmental goods and services as good as we received it from previous generations, and hopefully much better. This implies to account for benefits and costs over a long period of time, far into the future. This is not just philanthropy. This ethical imperative demands actions now, accompanied with various decisions, investments, policies, and programs. Significant resources have to spend now to yield adequate net benefits in the future.

The need to understand and self-realize that the Planet Earth is not a thing but a living entity.

The earth is a living being full of consciousness and life. The neoliberal system commodifies most elements of life, including nature. Sentient beings are things. The Earth is a big thing. This (reification) means that when we speak of sustainable development, we are speaking of relationships between a conscious being (the human being), with a bunch of things that do not have true life and true consciousness. This is not acceptable and, once human beings increase their levels of consciousness, this is not true. Every aspect of life on this planet is alive and possesses consciousness. When we self-realize that the Earth is a living being, the leader for sustainable development (this conscious leader) must walk a completely different road map! Sustainability as a collection of infinite interactions of various forms and levels of consciousness.

The imperative to define, in a collective and consensual way, the limits of human beings' interventions and transformation of nature.

How many more natural forests systems are to be depleted, to use wood in housing and furniture? Is there a limit? Who sets that limit and how is the limit respected? Also, until when will we continue to deplete our biodiversity, including all-natural species (flora and fauna)? Nobody should lead without at least being aware of this ethical dilemma. This is an ethical dilemma about sitting consumption, production and trade boundaries. The impacts of those activities go far beyond the physical buildings of governments and corporations. Similarly, the impacts of cutting the natural forest beyond a certain sustainable level, will affect every being over space and time.

The challenge we are facing with regard to the management of our global public goods.

These are the goods on this planet that belong to all of us as a collective humanity and sentient beings: climate, ozone layer, oceans, glaciers, water, air, mountains, peace, stability, security, and so on. How shall we manage these goods? How will the leaders of the future face and propose to manage these goods? This is a major ethical dilemma which is aggravated by the forms of governance that exist today on the global scene. For the moment, there is not a level of global consciousness so that our global public goods benefit all beings and not just a very few like today. Conscious leaders will have to emerge and propose solutions.

The recognition, quantification and settlement of the ecological debt between the developed and developing countries.

Most countries are not paying the true social and human costs of appropriating, using and depleting the natural resources of other countries, nor the embodied cost of pollution, climate change, and ozone layer depletion which have their origin in just a few countries. Parity must return and this debt is to be addressed comprehensively. This raises major issues of 'ecological justice', as many of the environmental problems are paired with social impacts of all sorts.

The great democratic deficit as a result of how international organizations function and how local environmental organizations are positioned in a given society.

International organizations are very much controlled by a handful of developed countries, and this creates a deficit when it comes to addressing problems and settle disputes. Examples abound within the UN context, the World Bank, and the World Trade Organization, just to name a few. The same situation happens in the countries, where the ministries of environment have no real traction or power to make the crucial decisions regarding development sustainability.

Furthermore, these ministries do not have decent budgets, adequate human resources, etc. A true environmental democracy must emerge from this new paradigm of conscious leadership. Today, this democracy is totally dominated by economics (economic values) and the market. Thus, we are seeing a major confrontation between Natural Law and the Law of the market, as these have very different sets of incentives, mechanisms, instruments, and declared behavior. The economic calculus must be merged with and ethics calculus; this is called *Ethicnomics*!

The asymmetric impacts of the negative-external-effects created as a result of production, consumption, trade, marketing, fear...

This asymmetry is born from the fact that the originating entity (the origin) of these negative externalities is not necessarily the same who has to bear the costs (the incidence). This happens everywhere, and has major ethical connotations as the origin often does not pay the costs of, for example, pollution. Where do the boundaries of a corporation or a country lie? Is it ethically correct to an upstream user of water to pollute the water for those downstream? Leadership will play a vital role in answering these moral and ethical questions.

The impacts of environmental deterioration and destruction of our social identity and our identity as a nation.

Changes in our natural resources, scenery, climate, and the like are great contributors to changes in social structures, inclusion and cohesion in our societies, neighborhoods, creation of communities, strengthening and empowerment of citizens, and rural existence. Sustainable development does not only include an economic change; sustainability embodies also major changes in the level and composition of our social capital: organizations, incentives, culture, human rights, traditions, etc., in addition to all aspects included in the 'human factor'. Destruction of our environment does not only ruin our material level of welfare but also progressively decays our spiritual well-being. We are not just another factor of production. We are conscious beings. It is unethical to impose only materially-based-criteria for decision making.

The negative impacts on our food and nutrition.

Every being has the right to clean and healthy food. This is a human right, as many others: civil and political rights, the right to life, the right to a clean environment, the right to education and health, the right to water, etc. Today, most of our foods are contaminated and, thus, they are not healthy. This is the result of using pesticides, herbicides, agrochemicals, additives, addictive substances, colorants, etc. Also, we are confronting serious issues with regards to the use of GMO seeds, because of the potential implications for our physical and mental health, and of the survival of local and indigenous people's communities.

The paradigm on leadership to be followed cannot avoid including ethical issues and concerns as an integral component. Three of them remain crucial to this new type of leadership:

1. Eco-Morality

The moral imperative of sustainable development forces us to think of a very different type of leader. To exercise leadership in a moral vacuum is the road to global disaster. All the attributes of sustainable development embrace a moral content, a moral challenge, a moral calculus. Not all is purely economics, material, and have more.

2. Ethicnomics

Economics and ethics have to be one, to be able to lead on matters such as global warming, biodiversity depletion, etc. The new leader will have to build the bridges between economics and ethics and create a new form of calculus for decision making: Ethicnomics. The ethics of economics and the economics of ethics.

3. Eco-Literacy

Sustainable leadership will not come about from one day to the other. One will have to create a social grammar, and a culture of sustainability. This is eco-literacy and should be an integral component of education, health, nutrition, and almost any human activity.

Consciousness for Ethical Leadership

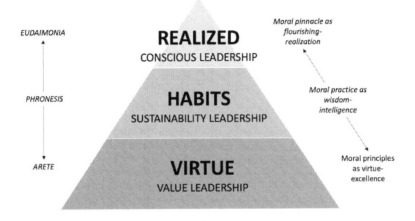

Figure 12: The Pyramid of Consciousness for Ethical Leadership

ETHICS OF SUSTAINABILITY AND LEADERS FOR PROSPERITY

Aristotle had envisioned the importance of realized conscious leadership called *eudaimonia*. It is a Greek word commonly translated as "happiness", "well-being" or prosperity but a more accurate translation would be "blessedness". This a moral pinnacle for flourishing and realization and a culminating level of consciousness. It can be achieved through the previous levels called *pronesis* and *arete*. Phronesis is a type of wisdom relevant to practical action sometimes referred to as "practical virtue". It is about moral practice as wisdom-intelligence in relation to habits for sustainability leadership and implies both good judgement and excellence of character. Arete is an ancient Greek word meaning excellence or virtue often used to signify the goal of education. If this is a trajectory for ethical leadership, what are the virtues, habits and self-realization journey necessary to leaders to become more effective in today's sustainability challenges? Ethics for sustainable development leadership is therefore developed and assessed along two trajectories. First, how do the leaders' personal/professional values align with the values and principles of sustainability? Second, how do the leader's executive/systemic capacity align with humanity's shared responsibility for the common good?

Before we address the characteristics that define leadership through sustainability practices and conscious awareness, we need to ask a couple of questions. What characteristics define the virtue and values for moral excellence in the context of sustainable development? What are the principles and organizational (corporate) conditions that would promote well-being and prosperity for all? The next two chapters will address these questions clarifying the principles of sustainability and the conditions for a sustainability-centered and socially responsible corporation.

CHAPTER X:
PRINCIPLES OF SUSTAINABLE DEVELOPMENT

"Earth provides enough to satisfy every man's need, but not every man's greed."
—Mahatma Gandhi

"Our biggest challenge in this new century is to take an idea that seems abstract - sustainable development - and turn it into a reality for all the world's people" **—Kofi Annan**

"Impermanence and selflessness are not negative aspects of life, but the very foundation on which life is built. Impermanence is the constant transformation of things. Without impermanence, there can be no life. Selflessness is the interdependent nature of all things. Without interdependence, nothing could exist." **—Thich Nhat Hanh,**

Many people think that those of us who lead on issues regarding sustainability are really arbitrary and biased in the way we make decisions (no hard decision criteria). This gets more prominent when one applies the Right Based

Approach to Development, and many see sustainability as a bundle of rights.

Those who are at the source of such criticism are the same people who argue that the economic criteria are basically neutral in impacts, unbiased in application, and universal in nature (are acceptable anywhere); and, it would yield results that have only positive impacts on people's well-being. In this context, some say that the negative impacts (i.e., the negative externalities) are an exception rather than a rule. That we only need to make some minor corrections at the margin (e.g., green taxes) in order to solve the situations in which they called exceptional.

The people addressing sustainability are not arbitrary. There are many principles and criteria which have been presented and explained for several decades, if not centuries. This chapter attempts to list some of these criteria, to illustrate the goodness and richness of a tremendous body of literature.

Principles and Criteria for Sustainable Development

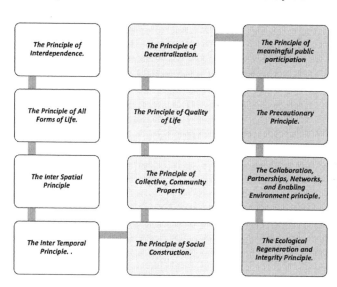

Figure 13: The Principles of Sustainable Development

SOME RELEVANT PRINCIPLES AND CRITERIA

These are principles that guide decisions on sustainability, which are essential to any possible definition of a leadership paradigm.

1. The Principle of Conservation as Opposed to Exploitation.

This principle has many definitions depending on the situation and the natural resource in question (renewable or non-renewable resource). One definition to retain is that conservation means to redistribute use rates over time towards the future. This is extremely instrumental not only in project evaluation but also in terms of macroeconomic changes (e.g., what is the impact on conservation from changes in national income, prices, taxation, subsidies, quotas, interest rates). Thus, this principle has a specific translation into macroeconomic policy making and the definition of use rates over space and time. Examples are the level and composition of government expenditures, the discount rates set by central banks, the instruments to raise government funds including green taxes, and much more.

2. The Principle of Interdependence.

This is one of the most fundamental principles in environment, ecology, resource economics, etc. This principle states that everything and everybody is interdependent in one form or another. We are all interdependent entities (human beings, sentient beings and nature). These days, there is no doubt in everyone's mind that we are interdependent with nature, not only in a material sense (thus, our material welfare), but also in a non-material (spiritual welfare) sense. This demands that countries, communities, and people in general cannot act as if they are independent or an island. The healing of the planet is indeed a fully interdependent process.

3. The Principle of All Forms of Life.

Most of the literature on environment and sustainable development is anthropocentric. The main concern is with us human beings. However, we know that human life is not the only one that counts in the road towards sustainable development. Thus, as stated earlier, sustainable leadership has to account for all forms of life, beings and sentient beings, and nature.

4. The Inter Spatial Principle.

The environmental phenomena do not resist or accept national boundaries. The concept of political boundaries is not relevant when dealing with global warming or ozone layer depletion, to name just two examples. Thus, notions of land management, zoning, assignment of property rights, and other instruments, are vital to govern space everywhere.

5. The Inter Temporal Principle.

The actions of today have great impacts in the future; be it the medium term of the long term. In fact, many actions of today may have lasting effects for many generations to come, like the elimination of the white rhinoceros from the planet and hundreds of animal and plant species.

6. The Principle of Decentralization.

In establishing policy instruments and programs for sustainable development, local actions, local communities and local governance play a crucial role. Notwithstanding the fact and the importance of global actions, globalization is not enough. Many advocates today 'glocalization', as the ultimate strategy: think globally and act locally. From the local to the global.

7. The Principle of Quality of Life.

Quantity and scale are not enough to human life. To have more is not necessarily better. More and more there is a greater emphasis on quality, and sustainable development is often seen as the road to quality.

8. The Principle of Collective, Community Property.

Sustainable development is mainly a call to collective action, cooperation, and solidarity. It is not about one person, one region or one country, even in situations we are addressing a local phenomenon. This demands a detailed revision of the relative importance of collective action, collective rights, and collective responsibilities.

9. The Principle of Social Construction.

Sustainable development is not just looking for some ecological balance and equilibrium. Sustainable development is also about creating and strengthening communities. This is a fundamental distinction with many other paradigms.

10. The Principle of Meaningful Public Participation.

This principle states that governments and markets are not the only mechanisms for the allocation of resources or the settlement of disputes. It states that citizens and non-governmental organizations play vital roles in decision-making. This is when empowerment becomes essential to attain the desired results.

11. The Precautionary Principle.

A fundamental principle that states something fundamental: one does not need to have all the scientific evidence to ac and make decisions. This principle has been approved by most countries of the world through the work of the United Nations. This is fundamental to take care of so many situations where science either does not provide the full evidence or shows controversial results.

12. The Collaboration, Partnerships, Networks, and Enabling Environment principle.

This principle is essential when addressing a collective concern. Today, collaboration is lacking and we see what the results are, for example, with regard to global warming, biodiversity depletion and the desertification of large areas of the world. This is the moment of partnerships of all the actors involved and of efficient and credible networks so that the world could be multiples and we all can heal the planet.

13. The Ecological Regeneration and Integrity Principle.

The healing process of the planet demands a series of processes, the principal of which are regeneration and integrity. This is to say, to regenerate ecological niches and situations that have decayed due to human activity. Ecological regeneration also as a source of growth, employment and development in general. Integrity refers to be able to respect creation and assume responsibility for its conservation, coherence, and equilibrium.

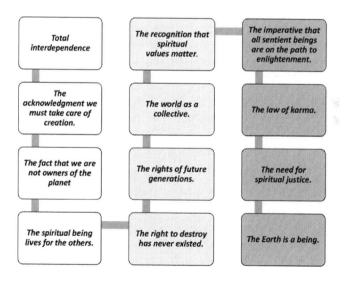

Figure 14: The Spiritual Principles of Sustainability

RELEVANT SPIRITUAL PRINCIPLES FOR SUSTAINABILITY

Behind every principle or human value there is one or more spiritual dimensions. There are important spiritual principles to be considered, some of which have been referred to before, like the principle of the totality of life: all forms of life have an inherent right to exist, and not just the human being. This right is given only by the fact that they are part of life on this planet. The emphasis here is in bringing to the fore the spiritual dimension that sustains the principle.

1. Total interdependence is key to spiritual growth and welfare.

All beings and all forms of life on our planet are interdependent. They are not independent. This type of interdependence has a purpose and a meaning; in other words, it is not random or spurious. Therefore, breaking the chain of interdependence means that many forms of life cannot evolve and transform as originally corresponds.

2. The acknowledgment we must take care of creation.

We have received the planet in a very well-defined way in terms of quantity and quality. We have received a portfolio of species and ways of life. We cannot give to future generations a planet whose state of life and wellbeing is inferior to that given to us. We, human beings, have the obligation to care for and preserve creation.

3. The fact that we are not owners of the planet.

We are part of the planet, with rights and responsibilities over everything that exists here. To conquer the planet is to conquer ourselves. To conquer higher levels of consciousness and responsibility. It does not mean enslaving other sentient beings.

4. The rights of future generations.

Future generations are intimately linked to us, as are past generations. We, the present generations, cannot limit the possibilities or abilities of self-realization of these future generations (it is not only about the satisfaction of material needs). It is a violation of your development and transformation rights. And, it is in that sense that these generations are subjects of right.

5. The right to destroy has never existed.

There is no right to destroy. There is no civilization, unless it has been sick, that accepts destruction for the sake of destruction. We must all be in favor of life with the diversity and great identity that it has.

6. The spiritual being lives for the others.

Many of us ask ourselves how to achieve salvation or how to attain enlightenment. The most accurate recipe is to dedicate yourself to the service of the other. And, if it is a spiritual form of service, better still. In Buddhism, this is called being a Bodhisattva: for whom the Buddhist path is the 'Buddha of All', including all forms of life.

7. The world as a collective.

We are not an island. We are a WHOLE. The world is not the sum of individuals. We are more than that. We belong to a form of collective of life, including human life. But we have a hard time identifying, designing, evaluating, and implementing the collective. Today, it is the era of collective spirituality. The spirituality of the other. Where my spiritual path is defined with and through the path of the other.

8. The recognition that spiritual values matter.

Everything needs a great revolution of values. Move from individualistic and materialistic values to spiritual, humanistic, and collective values: love, compassion, cooperation, solidarity, interdependence, justice, etc. These values are not words but states of being. You have to carry them out yourself. The bird learned them without going to university.

9. The imperative that all sentient beings are on the path to enlightenment.

Not only the human being is in the path of enlightenment; of its maximum expression in this earthly experience. All life forms are in the same process. Everything is a collective lighting. We are all on that path. A path of total mutuality: I am because you are, you are because I am. You have to walk together, without inflicting suffering.

10. The law of karma.

The law of karma is generally identified with the law of cause and effect. However, this law is also defined as the law of infinite equilibria; that is, 'at the end' all accounts must be settled. Therefore, the destruction of the planet, or of lives within the planet, has to be addressed. It is not a phenomenon outside of us but a reality within us. This is part of a new Eco-Morality and of making peace with the environment.

11. The need for spiritual justice.

Human justice is not like the so-called divine justice. But there is also a spiritual justice: to enter into the process of self-realization of the opposite. If I cause damage with the extraction, I must self-perform the conservation. If I cause harm it causes death damage, I must self-realize life.

12. The Earth is a being.

Transcendental spiritual experiences show that the planet Earth is not a collection of material things. It is a live entity that has its own dynamics as well as it contains all forms of life, including human lives. It has its live content, but it also acts as a live container.

These spiritual principles and dimensions are essential to understand who is a leader, what is leadership, and how to implement SL.

One cannot disregard these principles and, thus, one is also to focus on the spiritual dimensions of leadership. These are the true inner abilities of conscious sustainability leadership.

CHAPTER XI:
CORPORATION OF THE FUTURE

"To be truly successful, companies need to have a corporate mission that is bigger than making a profit." — **Marc Benioff, Salesforce**

"We have to bring this world back to sanity and put the greater good ahead of self-interest." — **Paul Polman, Unilever**

"Just as people cannot live without eating, so a business cannot live without profits. But most people don't live to eat, and neither must businesses live just to make profits." — **John Mackey, Whole Foods**

"Money motivates neither the best people, nor the best in people. It can move the body and influence the mind, but it cannot touch the heart or move the spirit; that is reserved for belief, principle, and morality." — **Dee Hock, Visa**

This is a transition section, before we address the leaders and the leadership. This transition is justified because many of the SL paradigms and programs are very much linked to (or surface from) the role of corporations and the private sector. Thus, we thought it was important to distill the anatomy of future corporations. And anatomy that must be compatible with our visions on sustainable development and leadership.

The attributes of the corporations of the future will be very different from the past. Herewith examples of some of the attributes this new corporation will embody:

1. The company will not feed itself only with profit-making.

The triple bottom line will be extremely important. It is not clear whether they know how to do it. It is not a matter of adding more. The economic calculus is different from the environmental and social calculus. Thus, the challenge to find an integrative framework capable of addressing these two calculi at the same time. This issue is very instrumental in making the links with the triangle of sustainability, and the possible ways sustainable leaders may contribute to the sustainability within and outside corporations. Without the private corporate sector, it will be impossible to attain the SDGs.

2. The company will have to make an important contribution to the collective welfare of the society where it is inserted.

This is a chapter in itself. But, suffice to say that the contribution of corporations will not only be on the private welfare of owners, managers and workers, and consumers. It must be a contribution to the whole collective welfare of a country, and the collective welfare of the planet. This is not a philanthropic quest; it is an obligation to do so.

3. The company will make a net contribution to the planet with carbon footprints close to zero.

To bring the carbon footprint to zero is the challenge to every actor in the economy. This path means structural changes in industry structures and processes, and a major shift pushed by technological change of the right type. Perhaps, the corporate world is just awakening to these major structural changes, and it has to take the initiative, as many automobile industries are pursuing at this point in time. Governments will not be able to do it by themselves.

4. The company will take care of one hundred percent of all its external negative effects, both social and environmental.

Corporations will take care of the whole cycle of their products and services. Thus, they will be responsible to produce, trade and recycle or recover any asset that either is part of their products or of a natural resource used in the process (land recovery out of mining). The hope is that the corporation will change the factor of production's composition towards sustainable production, trade and consumption. This means to internalize all externalities. Therefore, managerial attention will not only be internal to the company but also external, with recognition of their interdependence.

5. The company will be a space for self-realization.

Even if it is too trivial to say, corporations are people. Corporations exist because of people (owner, managers, workers, clients). Thus, being in a corporation it also means to 'live' in a corporation. Many hours of our lives are spent there, and therefore, it is vital that those hours be also a contribution to our own spiritual transformation; our inner self-realization. Productivity is not only determined by a given skill, but also it is determined by values, beliefs, experience, memory, social relations, trust, etc.

6. The company will be places for production, work, and for decent ways of life for all who act in it.

If one takes into account all the hours consumed by work and work-related activities, it is more than 50% of our lives. Thus, it is as if work is life and life is work. It is a way of life. As a way of life, it must contain all aspects of life and not just provide work services. In this sense, 'the work place' will be transformed in a 'life place': acceptable conditions, food and nutrition, recreation time, social relations and friendships, body-mind-soul care and development, and much more.

7. The company will consider innovation including both the business and the environment, inserted within the soul of all those involved.

All decision makers must create the incentives and the enabling environment to innovate. With what purpose? Is it just to increase the level of profits? It must go far beyond money or a material corporate goal. The corporation of the future will also care for innovative ways to protect and conserve the environment. But not only that; it would also be important to innovate in management styles, forms of human relations, types of works and work schedules, decent places of work, approaches to rest and leisure, family involvement, spiritual transformation and development. Innovation will not only be hardware but the expressions of many forms of software—material and non-material.

8. The company will not consider workers will not be factors of production but as collaborators (many forms of collaboration).

Many people see workers as 'labor', and labor as a factor of production. This is to transform a human being into a "thing", or simply a marketable commodity, with a price (wage). This approach is far away from what is coming in the future: workers as an essential point of collaboration, co-creation, etc. These will not be contracts but alternative forms of collaboration. A dramatic departure from the present. The organization of work will also become important, and workers will become part of a more integrated, fair, and coherent relationship. All workers will seek the practice of contemplative techniques as a key tool in the development of human capital. Also, labor organization will be much more participatory and oriented towards a new and renewed form of human capital.

9. The company will embrace eco-competitiveness for the benefit of all humanity.

This means an immaculate protection of the human and natural environment. Thus, this notion of competitiveness will change. At the moment, we use a dirty form of competitiveness, whereby the cost of negative externalities created by a given corporation are not embodied in the resources of that corporation. Often, it is the government that has to pay those external effects. The proposal and expectation here are that competitiveness will be transformed into "eco-competitive", where these external costs will be taken into account when evaluating any potential form of competitiveness. This will lead to an immaculate protection, conservation, of the human and natural environment.

10. The company will give priority to the social dimension, both in its responsibilities, allocation of resources, and implementation of specific activities.

The corporate sector will have to make a net positive contribution to social change and to resolve many social challenges in our society. Again, an important contribution of the private sector to public goods that emerge from social development: stability, inclusion, equity, human rights, integration, etc. Furthermore, and within the framework of sustainable development, we all must understand that the environmental crisis is often intimately linked to a social crisis. It is often practically impossible to separate the environmental from the social. Thus, corporations of the future will have to take this into account. Technology, innovation and strategic analysis will have greater unity and will be made available for business and social problems.

11. *The corporation will be less pyramidal and hierarchical and more horizontal and in matrix network.*

The integration will not be of physical characteristics or from top to bottom but of great virtual character. Challenges at a global level will be better calibrated and will consider local and domestic issues.

What would then be the nature of a sustainable corporation? Given all of the above here is a proposal of 12 points to consider:

1. Design the new corporate world and industrialization processes in terms of minimizing the use of non-renewable resources, the de-carbonization of productive processes, and the minimum use of fossil fuels.

2. Minimize the use of virgin and scarce raw materials, such as our native forests, glaciers, pristine waters, isolate ecological niches, etc.

3. Drastic reduction of waste generated and an increase in recycling and reuse by companies. The idea is to look for a different external effect.

4. Decrease to eliminate pollution of air, water and land. This has very important implications in relation to our agriculture, food, food processing, etc.

5. Re-align with the new concept of eco-competitiveness (see above), so that the negative and positive internal costs are in the calculations of the comparative and competitive advantages of all the companies.

6. Strongly strengthen the design and content of the corporate vision on sustainability, leadership...and that this new vision

is translated into the mission and the real purposes of the social and ecological.

7. Increase the capacity of long-term strategic planning, considering all the impacts in relation to the complete product cycle of different corporations and their scope.

8. Immediate creation of new markets or forms of production and distribution for the organic, clean products, nutritional strength, new ways of processing our food, clear and informative labeling.

9. Rational and coherent control and supervision of all suppliers and subcontractors in the ecological, environmental, human, decent work, fair wages, etc.

10. Creation and implementation of new indicators of economics, social and ecological efficiency, and social impact, reporting periodically on the carbon footprint and other important environmental indicators.

11. Realignment of all industrial processes to drastically reduce social and environmental impacts, including all corporate sectors, with a special emphasis on mining, forestry, agriculture, and the food industry.

12. Cause a great change of consciousness and corporations establish a new type of culture at national and international levels.

CHAPTER XII:
THE LEADERS: UNIVERSAL INGREDIENTS

"Knowing yourself is the beginning of all wisdom". — **Aristotle**

"Sustainable development is the pathway to the future we want for all. It offers a framework to generate economic growth, achieve social justice, exercise environmental stewardship and strengthen governance." — **Ban Ki-Moon**

"Leadership is the space and the road towards higher levels of awareness, concentration and consciousness of oneself, others, nature and spiritual reality." —**Alfredo Sfeir-Younis**

A t this moment in human history, the conscious leader we are all looking for, to lead and articulate the critical path towards sustainable development, will not only possess the attributes and ingredients of a general universal leader, but it will have to go much beyond that. The challenges and the intrinsic complexity of today's reality dictate so. There is no doubt that, in addition to the personal dimensions (the human factor) of a given leader, the uniqueness of the new leaders will be significantly determined by how one conceives "sustainable development". And, this is not a trivial proposition.

Example 1. If sustainable development is the attainment of a triple bottom line, then, not much beyond a general leader is needed. Some specific knowledge of the social and environmental dimensions of a given challenge might be needed. But that way of conceiving sustainable development has not brought societies to really address and attain the main objectives of a sustainable society. There is something missing in this particular concept of sustainable development.

Example 2. If one sees sustainable development as Gro Brundtland did, this opens new attributes and ingredients to a leader for sustainability. In particular, the capacity to understand what the long-term is all about. Specifically, that the long-term is not simply the arithmetic summation of various short terms. This is not a semantic issue. Conceiving, understanding, and addressing the long-term in any society is a very special activity; it has its own objectives, temperament, and identity. Today, economics and politics, for example, are dominated by short-term views and behaviors—i.e., benefits that accrue now are better than in the future. Money is worth more now (the whole debate on 'discount rates'). Not any leader has the capacity to establish actions and leadership for the longer-term. One of the prerequisites for this to happen is the construction of a totally new vision of human reality overtime. Yet another element of Brundtland's definition, which will shape the core attributes and contributions of this new leader, is the recognition of the rights future generations have today. This perspective is not just about age, or focusing on the youth, babies, or anything like that. What is required here is a leader with an immense capacity to identify and embrace societies which possess an infinite continuum of memory, wisdom, knowledge, and transformation processes, over long periods of human history. A leader that embodies an institutional memory shaped by very vast periods of time. A leader who is aware that we are to be connected to our origins, history, culture and experiences. We must be seeking a leader who sees goodness and positive grounds to a notion of life that exists within an infinite and diverse reality; a reality that must not be chopped by short-term events.

The same applies to the other notions and conceptions of sustainable development as outlined in earlier chapters; as a collection of values, as a bundle of rights, as a style of life, as a level of consciousness and so on.

Thus, we are faced with the recognition of those universal attributes of leaders, and those attributes derived from our understanding of sustainable development.

This is why we will distinguish between two types of attributes of a leader for sustainable development. The first group of attributes will be labeled Important Universal Ingredients. The second group, at the end of this chapter, will identify attributes that are unique to sustainable development leaders, based on a specific notion of sustainability (i.e., Conscious Development), labeled Secret Ingredients.

IMPORTANT UNIVERSAL INGREDIENTS

In focusing on these universal ingredients of a new leader, we will find many definitions, opinions and controversies about leaders.

But, before we address each and every ingredient, it is important to preamble that dimension clarifying an important and controversial issue. This issue addresses leadership in the context of citizens' sovereignty. Many people pose the question of whether one needs leaders in the first place. We assume that this question refers to an old traditional paradigm of "one leader, and millions of followers". Something very egocentric and hierarchical in nature. In this paradigm, a leader means one person who exercises leadership over a large group, which is supposed to follow. In today's world, where the grassroots movements are growing and empowering most citizens, fewer activists favor the 'one leader' approach. They either see each person as a leader or the whole community as a leader; everyone at the same level in decision-making. All those involved with the same level of empowerment, and thus no 'one leader'. Many youth organizations do not function with a linear or hierarchical model of leadership, which includes "some leaders and many followers".

This is neither a question of quantity nor a question of hierarchical structures. They see the debate on leadership as a major change in the economic, political and social paradigm of development and human transformation. In a recent poll we made through Facebook, about the type of leader we need in order to heal the planet, some respondents said that I should not even use the word "leader". That this word was anachronistic. This view should not be disregarded.

However, for the purpose of this book, we will continue to use the term 'leader', although we are not saying anything about numbers or the mechanisms necessary to lead in a particular way or direction. This will be the subject of the next chapter on leadership.

There is no doubt that the literature on sustainable leadership has borrowed many attributes of leaders that have been presented in the areas of management, psychology, and political science. These attributes are more or less universal and, thus, they will be instrumental in the design and implementation of the SL paradigm as well.

Examples of these attributes were given above, and they will not be repeated here (e.g., committed, resilient, compassionate, listener, integrity, visionary, effective communicator, persuasive, generous, motivator, creative, flexible, dedicated...). The list is very long. And, as we change our notions of development and transformation, these attributes keep coming. Here, the emphasis will be on those attributes that are indispensable to those who are to lead on sustainable development (this section) and, then, on empowered and conscious development (next section).

CSL Universal Ingredients

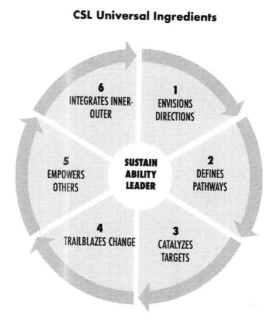

Figure 15: Universal Ingredients of Sustainability Leadership

Examples of Important Universal Attributes that will make the SL a unique paradigm.

1. Envisions Directions

The leader is one who is supposed to know the direction of change and transformation. This is why it was vital to discuss first the meaning and scope of sustainable development. One needs to know sustainability in its totality to define the 'direction of change' the leader will put forth to the rest of the people. Otherwise, where and how is the leader going to lead? How does the leader know the direction to be followed?

2. Defines Pathways

The leader must know how to define 'reality' in order to map out the nature of the leadership and the path to follow. Reality is always changing, and sustainability is to cope with these realities. To define reality means to define a new vision. It is to identify clearly the intent of leadership. It means to create a language that will agglutinate all concerns behind a clear strategy and a path to be followed. Once it knows, the leader shows the path.

3. Catalyzes Targets

The leader must understand the common objective or purpose to be attained. Once the vision is clear, this vision needs to be articulated and translated into specific objectives. Otherwise, there will be no coherent actions. The SDGs defined by the UN is one important example of such objectives. Here, the term 'common' refers also to the 'desires' and the 'expectations' of men and women who are looking for leadership. In a sense, this attribute underlines the individual and collective nature of the vision and the leadership which corresponds to that vision. It is a totally symbiotic relationship. It does not take people where only the leader wants to go, but it takes the people where they want to go (collective vision). A leader sometimes must take the people where they do not want to go.

4. Trailblazes Change

The leader is often seen as an influencer of the most powerful decision makers. For many people, sustainability of development involves a power structure that needs to be changed and modified. The ownership and use of natural resources and the services of the environment are a major source of power in our society. And, it is within this environment of power that the leader for sustainability will have to intervene. The leader must be aware of this equation of power.

5. Empowers Others

The leader is key to any process of empowerment. Including inner and outer empowerment. To be a leader for sustainability not only means to empower oneself, but to be someone who is capable and willing to empower others. In sustainable development leadership is a process of empowering individuals, communities, regions, countries... Empowerment is an attribute with individual and collective ingredients. One of the great failures in sustainable development projects and programs has been the lack of empowerment of the communities that are affected by a road towards sustainability.

6. Integrates Inner-Outer

The true leader for sustainability is capable of establishing the core of leadership in the 'inner' and in the 'outer'. The outer means the material reality we are living into. The inner means the reality we face in our inner souls. It is essential to recognize both aspects of leadership, and address the issues discussed earlier about the 'spiritual dimensions' of sustainability. It is essential to have the capacity to lead from within; something of vital importance. There is no outer leader without the existence of an inner leader. Something very much missing.

CHAPTER XIII:
THE LEADER: SECRET INGREDIENTS

"Be a global citizen. Act with passion and compassion. Help us make this world safer and more sustainable today and for the generations that will follow us. That is our moral responsibility." **–Ban Ki-Moon**

"Humankind has not woven the web of life. We are but one thread within it. Whatever we do to the web, we do to ourselves. All things are bound together. All things connect." **– Chief Seattle**

"The great attribute of a leader is to transcend and contain levels ever higher of individual and collective consciousness." **– Alfredo Sfeir-Younis**

Now, let's turn to the secret and unique ingredients of the leaders who will indeed take all of us to a sustainable society and to heal the planet.

To address these secret ingredients, we have to recall the notions of sustainability and sustainable development that give shape and form the basis for these attributes. From an above section, we believe in sustainable development as:

1. A post-era and transition from socioeconomic development and a preamble to conscious and empowered development,

2. A collection of unique values,

3. A bundle of collective rights and the right to development, and

4. A style of life. Thus, we have to identify the attributes against these dimensions of sustainability.

These notions open the spaces for the following secret ingredients:

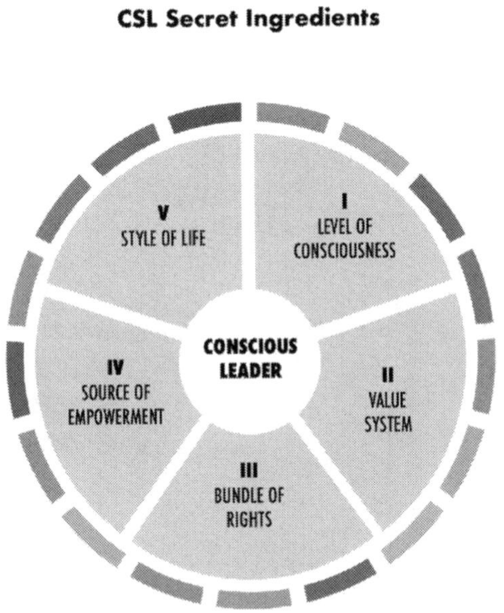

CSL Secret Ingredients

Figure 16: Secret Ingredients of Conscious Leadership

I. SUSTAINABILITY AS A LEVEL OF CONSCIOUSNESS

THE CONSCIOUSNESS: ALL BECOMES ONE

1. High levels of human consciousness

The world reveals in front of leaders in many different and complex ways. This puts a leader within the permanent realm of decisions, and in the unique position to establish proper responses to others. Most leaders are faced with at least two realms of decisions: resolve problems and predict the future, and those combined, guide others into the future. We live in complex times, and we all have different experiences in life and, thus, very different narratives of those experiences. The experiences, how one lives them, and the intensity embedded within them, all define those narratives. This resulting narrative is an expression of human consciousness (nature, level, manifestation). In many respects, how you look at something, how do you end up defining the world around you, and how you decide and become a true creator of your destiny and the destiny of others depends on the attributes and levels of your consciousness. Furthermore, as a leader one needs the least of biases and the least of impartial judgements to understand reality, individually and collectively.

Leaders have to cultivate their consciousness and awareness to become less random in their behavior, advice and projections. The complexity of the world (including governments, enterprises, and citizens' organizations) demands the realization of ever higher values in decision making. Consciousness is the container and the co-creator of embracing and using those higher values. The global nature of human existence today implies to have leaders who hold more universal perspectives with little load from self-interest, and suggest proper responses to others (the collective). Finally, one cannot disregard the importance of connection with nature; an ever-sophisticated realm of interdependent realities. This is particularly true for leaders who will face conscious decisions regarding sustainable development.

2. Self-realization of all forms of interdependence

The self-realization of interdependence is the essence of leaders for the 21st Century. Leaders of a new future will have to master all forms of interdependence: among human beings, sentient beings and nature, and the spiritual DNA of all forms of life. Nobody and nothing are independent. That is an illusion. Also, no person is an island and, thus, we cannot convert leadership into a process of human and social fragmentation. Some leaders do in order to gain power in corporations or governments. This is the element of connectivity in leadership and, thus, a fundamental attribute of a leader. To be permanently aware of interdependence –people, regions, countries, corporations, citizens, etc. is the key to awareness, mindfulness, and purpose. Any element of disconnection will in many ways interrupt leadership, or will generate unacceptable outcomes of human actions. The leader cannot be disconnected from people and nature, and a reconnection to full interdependence is an important attribute of a conscious sustainability leader. Thus, part of the leader's efforts must be devoted to reconnect to everyone who is to be led. It is through interdependence that leadership will affect the container (e.g., planet, corporations, governments, institutions) and the content of everyday life (e.g., human beings, sentient beings).

3. Self-realized in the collective values of transformation

The decisions we make are the result of the values and belief system we hold. In the neoliberal and market-oriented system, individualistic and materialistic values are those that count. Examples are competition, concentration of wealth, and exclusion, in which everyone tries to maximize its own welfare independent of others. The law of the most powerful, guided by wealth and purchasing power. Contrary to this, sustainable development, with an empowered citizenship, gives special importance to collective values. Examples are cooperation, collaboration, solidarity, interdependence, justice, equity, love, compassion, etc. The process of self-realization of these values do transform the individual and the collective in very special ways. Leaders for sustainable development will be the principal holders of these collective values, if conservation and proper management of natural resources and the services of the environment are to happen in practice. No leadership will be legitimate without this self-realization. True leaders transform, and this process of transformation has direct relevance in relation to these collective values.

4. Transcend space and time

A distinct preoccupation of those in the field of sustainable development is to correct the existing "externalities". This is to say, to correct the negative external effects of corporations, government and citizens. An example of such externalities is air and water pollution as a result of corporate processes and alternative forms of wealth creation. There are spatial (when the upstream users of a river contaminate the water to be used by downstream users) and inter-temporal externalities (when this generation over-exploit the planet earth leaving little or nothing to the future generations). Sustainable development is, in a sense, the art of governing actions over space and time. The concept of "conservation" has its essence in the management of time: moving use rates of a given natural resource into the future. The farther into the future those rates move, the higher the rate of conservation of that natural resource. Thus, conscious leaders for sustainability will have to master and transcend space and time, and have an eye view of totality in a holistic way. This is an essential attribute so that leaders do not get mesmerized with simple and immediate short-term gains.

5. Inner self-empowerment

Many people empower themselves by "having more" (more is better); particularly possessing more material things. For them, the principle of "more is better" applies everywhere. This is an "outer form of empowerment". This is so pervasive that even modern economics and corporate performance are measured by how they comply or attain external and material indicators. We also find this outer form of empowerment marking the difference among corporate owners and managers. An example of this is Forbes Magazine, which shows a leadership concept based on material wealth. Nothing could be further from the truth. The true leader of the 21st Century will also be empowered through the inner self: consciousness, awareness, mindfulness, meditation, contemplation, silence, prayer, etc. This applies to the individual and collective manifestations of leadership. This also applies to workers, followers or any individual in society. It is the inner empowerment process, the one which is going to strengthen the leader's consciousness, intelligence, memory, wisdom, etc. Inner empowerment is vital to leaders of today and the future.

6. Possesses a powerful discriminating and non-discriminating mind

Everyone needs a discriminating mind, to be able to choose at all times between one scenario and another, one road to travel or another or, one decision or another. The quality of those choices will depend on the quality and level of consciousness embodied in one's discriminating mind. Low level of consciousness will translate into weak or inadequate decisions. Many professions are the foundation, and often exacerbate the development and use of the discriminating mind. This exacerbation implies the atrophy of the non-discriminating mind. Simply, the mind of what it is. Many times, things are the way they are and the leader is not there to change it. Sometimes leaders are blind of what it is, and impose what it should be and, unfortunately, acceptance is not part of leadership. The point here is that the conscious leader must be aware of both, what it is and what it should be. High levels of consciousness on both the discriminating and non-discriminating mind.

II. SUSTAINABILITY AS A VALUE SYSTEM

THE POWER OF LEADING RIGHT

7. Representative of, and engaged into, the ethics and morals for sustainability and integrity. Uncover the truth and do not hide it.

Leaders must be transparent. Followers demand that. It is not just a moral principle, but it is a unique requirement by those who are willing to be led. This is why conscious leaders must have the attribute of uncovering the truth and not hiding it. But what is the truth? Perhaps, each leader, each person will hold its own truth, as dictated by their corresponding levels of consciousness. In part, this question will never be answered. It might not be possible. But it does not invalidate the importance of addressing this crucially important question. The power of leading right means the road towards a 'collective truth'; a truth that will ring the bell with the large majority that trust the conscious leader. The collective truth manifests in many different ways, and the conscious leader must be able to contain it, work with it, and use its energy to create a new awakening on the large majority of people. The conscious leader is the bridge that becomes the processor of that collective truth which will lift up all into a new level of collective consciousness.

8. Knows righteousness and the limits.

The term 'righteousness' has several meanings that are essential attributes to the conscious leaders. In general, it represents something or a behavior that is morally correct, morally justified, honest and legitimate, represents a duty and proclaims justice, with integrity and virtue. In Buddhism, it encompasses also noble, pure and charitable, within some agreed moral code of conduct. Leaders must be in right and harmonious relationships with others, so that one may justify leadership activities. There must be a superior objective to act right, like love, compassion and peace. The social meaning of righteousness also encompasses to assist people who are in need, and conscious leadership becomes an opportunity to serve people. It is essential that conscious leaders embody and practice righteousness all the time. This practice will set the limits to leadership, and will establish a clear metric of good and bad forms of leadership.

III. SUSTAINABILITY AS A BUNDLE OF RIGHTS

LIFE IS A PRACTICE

9. Understands the rights of all beings and sentient beings and nature

One of the greatest transformations most societies are going through is a move towards less markets and more rights. Not only Civil and Political Rights (freedom, non-discrimination, right to vote), but also the Economic, Social and Cultural Rights (right to clean water and sanitation, righto education and health), and The Right to Development (no one can constrain my capacities to develop as a person, as a community or as a country). In the area of sustainable development, all forms of rights are extremely relevant, as they will define access, ownership, use and management of all-natural resources and the services of the environment. The assignment of rights is a key instrument of economic and social policy from the perspective of either corporations, governments and citizens. Leaders must fully understand the importance of the existing bundle of rights, as these define all the processes of wealth creation, wealth allocation and distribution, and all forms of conservation and management. However, conscious leaders must also be aware that these rights not only apply to human beings, but also to sentient beings and nature. Today, one of the key constitutional reforms is that of assigning rights to nature, and deposit the responsibilities on us human beings. The rights of animals, forest protection, and productivity of the oceans are also important examples of avenues that are to follow for the conscious leaders for sustainability.

10. Embodies a style of life that is unique and an example to all.

Sustainable development is also about choosing a style of life that is harmonious with Natural Law and the wellness of the planet. We are aware that the present style of life imposed by economic globalization has accelerated the rates of resources depletion everywhere. Quality of life for many people is not really acceptable or desirable. People are demanding that the leaders of the future somehow embody a style of life that may serve as an example to all those who are following. This means that leaders for sustainability must be fully coherent with the principles of sustainable development. Leaders must lead by example. This is an important attribute, particularly when exercising leadership within the human collective.

11. Spiritual Being

Sustainable development is not only about attaining high levels of material welfare, but also high levels of spiritual welfare. Many constitutions around the world recognize both forms of welfare. In the end, a significant equilibrium must exist between the two forms of welfare. To understand the meaning of spiritual welfare, it is essential to develop one's own spirituality: the path towards the inner self. All of us are seeking more than just material possessions. We are seeking, for example, happiness, joy, satisfactions, etc.

Conscious leaders must be spiritual in nature. To be spiritual in this context means to care and love others; to care about people, animals and nature. Conscious leaders must self-realize that we are One, and honor in every action the power of Oneness in this immense diversity. Conscious leaders must not strive for possessions but for the self-realization of human values and a virtuous all-inclusive sustainable development.

12. Powerful healer

Leading right is a powerful form of healing. Thus, conscious leaders must be powerful healers. This means to have the attributes of listening, consistency, knowing those who are being led, embodying positive emotions, ability to diagnose the situation well, having detailed knowledge of the causes and conditions, having the ability to transcend the immediate, etc. Furthermore, a powerful healer as a conscious leader must be highly sensitive to the natural and human environment, possess a broad vision, very aware of the interconnectedness of all with all, and very clear on what are the limits that should not be violated. This healing attribute of the conscious leader demands a very close connection with the people, moving beyond the five senses, and being aware of the place one is located on the road to the collective horizon.

IV. SUSTAINABILITY AS A SOURCE OF EMPOWERMENT

OUR COLLECTIVE INTERDEPENDENT NATURE

13. Lives humanity as a collective

While leadership may be exercised by an individual person, its essence is collective. There is always one more entity to lead or to follow. As has been expressed several times in this book, the true meaning of the collective goes beyond human beings. Leadership for sustainable development is not an anthropocentric concept. The collective includes human beings, sentient beings and nature. This is why the conscious-sustainability-leader must live humanity as a collective; as an expanded collective. This attribute is not self-evident because it is necessary that one is to reach a high level of consciousness to be able to experience and understand that sentient beings and nature are equally alive. It is not an act of faith or a slogan; it is an inner and outer experience. Humans have a natural body and a natural mind that guide us from the inner to the outer, in our relations with nature. Even the spiritual path of an individual is always immersed in the collective. Nothing is separable. This unity we are talking about belongs to a space and level of consciousness, where there is an interdependent unity with everyone and everything. This state of consciousness is another attribute of this conscious leader.

14. Bastions of all forms of cooperation and collaboration

Because we live in a collective, it becomes imperative also to establish the foundation for all forms of collaboration and cooperation among all the possible actors involved. The leader should have the inner space to identify, register and store all forms of collaboration among those who have different views of life. This is immersed in diversity and various manifestations of leader and follower relationships, public or private. Leadership should be a unifying force and leaders should be the bridges so that union may take place. Leaders not only will have to self-realize collaboration and cooperation, but also be the vehicle for those attributes to become important features of the public domain and all forms of decision making. In today's world, and within the realm of sustainability, there is an ever-increasing power of citizens. Markets, governments, corporations of politics are not any longer the key variables. To lead in the space of citizenship will not be easy and it will demand lots of collaboration.

15. They lead so others can encounter their own mission, purpose, identity and goals in transformation. Non-obstructions to others.

Leadership does not consist in demanding others to be like the leader. That is a wrong form of leadership. The true act of a real leader is to act in a way that others may find their mission on this planet. To find their own selves. To find the reason why they are on this planet, at this very moment in history. Leaders are not like a dam. They are the ones that should let every river flow in the direction dictated by their own nature. Thus, lead so that others may encounter their own missions, their own mandates, their own Dharmas. The triumph of a conscious leader comes about when he/she was able to allow others to encounter their own purpose in life, and not the purpose of the leader, where the "other" is the essence of leadership. This attribute demands immense awareness of the true path of human transformation. That is why we need self-realized leaders, and not obstructionist leaders. Today, many unconscious leaders impose their identity and purpose. Even in the literature about the best trades of leaders there is a bias regarding certain attributes of leaders. Peoples have their own attributes to become fully self-realized. The instrument is the conscious leader.

16. It is a container and a refuge for everyone

Most people need to have a unique corner in their lives. This may be in the privacy of their own home, or a special place in nature. Also, people need a special refuge in the public domain, despite being surrounded by millions of people. The conscious leader must become the container of all forms of refuge in the public spaces. The conscious leader is a very unique container. For those of us who have been in a leadership position, we know what that container truly is. To be the container takes lots of work and inner capacity. One becomes de facto the container of the questions and the answers; the container of the inner and the outer; the container of the true and the false; the container of the individual and the collective; the collective of the quantity and the quality. If the leader is not the container, very soon will see the leadership position eroded, disregarded, and depleted. Without a spiritual path to expand one's own inner container, it will be rather difficult, if not impossible, to lead. Mastering this attribute takes time as it is based on the first spiritual law: "The Law of Spiritual Space". This law states that "all states of being occupy space", be them positive (love) or negative (anger, greed). Conscious leadership is not only about contents, but it is also about containers.

17. Seva: Service and philanthropy for a greater cause

True conscious leaders do not do 'a job'. They do 'service' to humanity. When you lead, you are not going to 'work'. You are going to serve. A very big difference. Attitude towards work (a minimizing attitude) is very different than toward service (open, ready and available). In doing work, you expect an outcome. You do work to make money, for example. In doing Seva you expect nothing. You do it without expectations for recognition. The ego is completely out of a Seva based leader. In Hinduism, this is called Seva, and it is said by the great masters that the most effective way to reach enlightenment is via Seva. But, Seva demands actions, establishes identity, and creates bridges among diverse groups of people. Seva in Christianity is closely related to the notion of servant leadership. In indigenous traditions Seva is expressed in the notion of "cargo" as a responsibility and role for the common good of the community. In the Seva the most important is to lead a greater cause. Not necessarily the cause of the leader. This is a unique attribute of the conscious leader, as awareness must be focusing on the totality and not be manipulated by self-interest.

18. They are fully connected with our ancestors and indigenous cosmovision

Ancestry is a key attribute of conscious leaders. In essence, it means to be connected to the origin. What origin? The origin of leadership: the core of the mind, body and soul. But, also, in practice it means to be connected with your ancestors, those who led in the past. This is key in the pursuit of sustainable development: the harmony with nature. The indigenous peoples' cosmovision is a foundation for what all conscious leaders may do for sustainability. A unified vision of nature and man. Now, fractured by the economic, social and political systems. People have an origin, otherwise they will not have a destination. Conscious leaders are those who assist people in getting closer and closer to their destiny. Walking towards collective destiny is the most challenging issue at this moment in human history.

V. SUSTAINABILITY AS A STYLE OF LIFE

Humanness: One with the Planet

19. Knows and realizes the Planet is a living entity. Sees life everywhere.

Most people and paradigms on leadership assume that the planet is "a thing" like a collection of raw materials and it is not really a live entity. Leading or managing things is very different from managing live entities, like human beings, sentient beings, and nature. This is a fundamental leadership principle today. Nature has energy, and we know that. Because it has energy, it is alive (all our fruits and vegetables are alive; otherwise, dead food leads to death!). Because the earth is alive, it has memory (an apple tree gives apples and not oranges). And, because it has memory, it has consciousness (possesses many levels of awareness). A conscious planet is the essence of the new sustainable development paradigm explained earlier: Conscious Development. In essence, these attributes open leadership to a constant interaction of all expressions of consciousness, the consciousness of the leader, the people are trying to lead, the consciousness of all sentient beings and the consciousness of nature. This is the true meaning of the "conscious leader": an ability to attain higher and higher levels of consciousness. Leadership will never take place between a "conscious entity" and a "dead entity". This is simply not possible. Basically, leadership is an expression of consciousness in the first place, and can only be applied within a space of consciousness. It is not a riddle; it is the foundation for an essential attribute of a leader.

20. Embodies an equilibrium of all elements of life: water, air, space, earth and fire.

Life is composed of five elements: water, earth, wind, space, and fire. If life is composed of those elements, then, a live leadership must be linked also to those elements as strange as that may first sound. In sustainable development, where also nature is at the center of the attention, to give emphasis to the linkages between the five elements of life and leadership is crucial. These linkages will be more apparent and better experienced, when one understands and practices a fundamental spiritual law, "the outer is like the inner and the inner is like the outer". In other words, leaders for sustainability must focus on both, the inner ecology and the outer ecology of life. Inner environment and outer environment, they are inseparable. They are fully interdependent. Thus, essential to sustainability leadership is to attain a very solid equilibrium among all the elements of life. Conscious sustainability leaders will have to be fully engaged on the availability, quantity, and quality of these five elements of life, they will have to also be aware of those elements inside their own lives. This demands training on the self-healing processes necessary to heal the inner ecology, and through the cleaning of their inner ecology, clean also the outer ecology. This is a theme that demands a book in itself.

21. The long-term. Leaders of The Time Element

Many leaders operate only for short term results, and when they are put in a situation to lead for the construction of a long-term horizon they do not act, accordingly. Thus, governments do the same, corporations do the same, and most institutions and institutional arrangements do the same. Clearly, and reality confirms this, the longer term is not the linear addition of short terms. It is a totally different realm of reality. It needs to be constructed and developed so that long-term aims and goals are attained (e.g., the SDGs). This short-term bias is tragic, particularly when we are to operate in the realm of sustainability and sustainable development. The conservation and management of natural resources and environmental services are to be applied with the long-term in mind. The true leader must be able to embed time in all its dimensions and not only pay attention to the immediate. Today, we see with great consternation how difficult it is to put leadership at the service of climate change and biodiversity depletion, to use only two examples. Leadership to find harmonic and coherent ways to construct a future for all generations, including future generations, is a very scarce commodity. This is in essence the secret of time in management, economics and public policy.

22. They are true accordions of the past and future into present time: Mindful Leaders

It is not possible to conceive leaders who are not living in full awareness. Awareness of the present time (mindfulness), the past time, and the future time. Past time is essential because it stores a huge institutional and historical memory. Leaders cannot act disconnected from the experiences of the past; otherwise, they will continue exercising a mediocre leadership and repeating the mistakes of the past. Obviously, the term leader embeds somehow the architecture and the foundations towards a new future. If not, there will be no need for leaders. This has to do with the earlier discussion over long-term issues and concerns. But it is essential that a leader be fully aware of the present time. It is imperative that a leader is a self-realized person on mindfulness: an ability, an experience and a process of self-realization of present reality. The sustainability leaders must have the awareness of an accordion: to fold the future and the past into present time, all the time. This is an ability that must be developed through contemplative techniques and through very sophisticated and programmed experiences.

CSL Integrated and Comprehensive Model

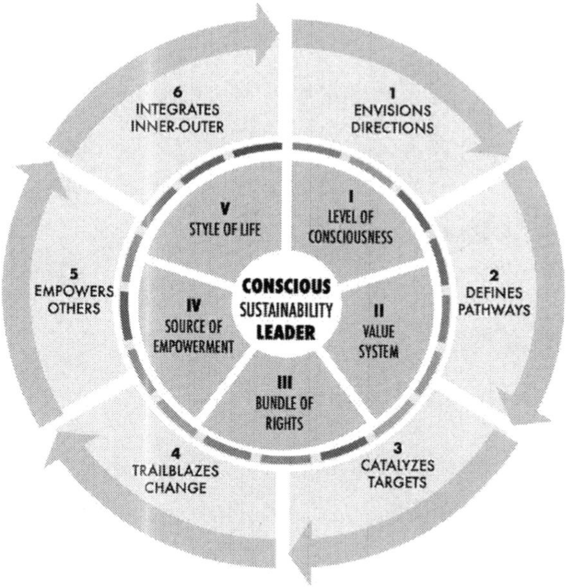

Figure 17: CSL Integrated Model

BOX 3: SUMMARY OF THE CSL DIMENSIONS

I. Sustainability as a Level of Consciousness

The Consciousness: All Becomes One

1) High levels of human consciousness

2) Self-realization of all forms of interdependence

3) Self-realized in the collective values of transformation

4) Transcend space and time

5) Inner self-empowerment

6) Possesses a powerful discriminating and non-discriminating mind.

II. Sustainability as a Value System

The Power of Leading Right

7) Representative of, and engaged into, the ethics and morals for sustainability and integrity. Uncover the truth and not hide it.

8) Knows righteousness and the limits.

III. Sustainability as a Bundle of Rights

Life is a Practice

9) Understands the rights of all beings and sentient beings and nature.

10) Embodies a style of life that is unique and an example to all.

11) Spiritual Being

12) Powerful healer

IV. Sustainability as a Source of Empowerment

Our Collective Interdependent Nature

13) Lives humanity as a collective.

14) Bastion of all forms of cooperation and collaboration.

15) They lead so others can encounter their own mission, purpose, identity and goals in transformation. Non-obstructions to others.

16) It is a container and a refuge for everyone.

17) SEVA: service and philanthropy for a greater cause.

18) They are fully connected with our ancestors and indigenous cosmovision.

V. Sustainability as a Style of Life

Humanness: One with the Planet

19) Knows and realizes the Planet is a living entity. Sees life everywhere.

20) Embodies an equilibrium of all elements of life: water, air, space, earth and fire.

21) The long-term. Leaders of The Time Element.

22) They are true accordions of the past and future into the present time. Mindful leaders. The 8-fold path. Concentration.

CHAPTER XIV:
LEADERSHIP, SUSTAINABILITY AND COLLECTIVE EMOTIONS

"Fill your bowl to the brim and it will spill. Keep sharpening your knife and it will blunt. Chase after money and security and your heart will never unclench. Care about people's approval and you will be their prisoner. Do your work, then step back. The only path to serenity."

— Lao Tzu

"To handle yourself, use your head; to handle others, use your heart."

— Eleanor Roosevelt

"I've learned that people will forget what you said, people will forget what you did, but people will never forget how you made them feel."

— Maya Angelou

"Leadership and learning are indispensable to each other."

–John F. Kennedy

There is an important connection between leadership and emotions, and between collective emotions and sustainable development (i.e., healing the planet). The theme of collective emotions is also relevant as regards leadership education and training, and in defining the academic curriculum of leadership for sustainability programs.

The attention to collective emotions, and not to individual emotions (behavior, action, and individual effort), is also something to note here. Leaders will have to be prepared to navigate and orient communities, unions, corporations, countries and global citizens; all of which having energies, memory, emotions, wisdom, and consciousness.

It is clear that there is an emotional dimension of a leader, or any person for that matter. However, the emphasis here will be on how leaders are capable of creating and changing collective emotions, and how collective emotions affect leaders. Since we are addressing sustainable development, the effort here is to highlight the relationship between collective emotions and the state of the planet. It is a two-way street: nature may affect collective emotions and collective emotions may affect nature.

These are major themes which must be included into any discussion or paradigm on leadership.

When addressing collective emotions, it is important to define clearly what does a collective include? Our definition of "collective" goes far beyond human beings; it includes all human beings, sentient beings, and nature. This definition, in itself, represents a great paradigm shift. In particular, it demands to focus, for example, on collective emotions, collective motional education, and collective healing of the planet.

Thus, this chapter outlines what may become a central conscious leadership's issue, where leaders must also understand emotions, address emotions, self-realize emotions, and lead emotions. We will outline the mosaic of a new dimension of the CSL paradigm, including references to "emotional education".

It is essential to make explicit the hypothesis that on the one hand, the destruction of the planet –an absence of sustainability– is a great source of collective emotions and, on the other hand, some collective emotions are a great source of destruction of the planet. Something that goes in both directions. Thus, the destruction of the planet must be central to any debate on "emotional education" and the formation of leaders. We know that the progressive ecological depletion creates great collective emotions, such as fear, uncertainty, loss of identity and the sense of belonging, competition, exclusion, concentration, etc.

It is evident today that collective emotions surface as a result of climate change: rains, hurricanes, tsunamis; loss of biodiversity (plants, animals, insects); water and air pollution (lack of physical and mental health); ecological weakening of the planet; water scarcity (war on water); and the loss of oceans' productivity.

All the above may also be seen through the impacts of these ecological and emotional states on illnesses, now called environmental diseases (environmental medicine). This raises an infinite number of questions leaders have to address: can't there be a healthy human being on a sick planet? How do we address the emotions of sentient beings –going beyond just human beings?

Some suggest that the great problem resides in the nature and quality of our education. It may be so. Thus, if we offer education as the solution we must differentiate among different forms of education. There are several types of education:

Cognitive Education (traditional).

This is the education of the mind. If this is the only type of education offered, the education is incomplete. It is relevant to add that we have many minds; one of which is "the natural mind". This mind has a direct relationship with nature. Conscious sustainability leaders must recognize and develop their natural minds. A highly developed natural mind will be able to heal through nature.

Emotional Education.

This is not only the psychology of a person's emotions (there is a lot of that). No, one needs an emphasis on the collective nature of emotions, and the need to have an educational system that is able to address those collective emotions. Its collective dimension is given by the power of relationships that exist (i) with oneself, (ii) with the other, (iii) with others, and (iv) with everything and everyone. Again, emotional education does not end human relationships. It includes relationships with all sentient beings and nature. Animal abuse as an example.

Body Education.

The body is as wise and intelligent as the mind and the soul. The body has its own language, but we know very little about it. Pain, tiredness, temperature...as one of the forms of expression of the body. The body is a map of information. That is the reason why the success of bio-dance. Just as there is a natural mind, there is also a natural body, which is the bridge between the physical body and nature. Leaders must listen to their bodies and capture the wisdom embedded there as a very powerful instrument of leadership.

Spiritual Education.

A holistic approach to leadership demands a holistic approach to leadership. And, this means the education of the body, mind and soul. Spiritual education is often identified with this holistic dimension. At a subtler level, some may experience the great interdependence that exists among all our missions on this planet

(Dharmas). This is critical for leaders who understand leadership as a vehicle for the enlightenment and highest level of consciousness of themselves and those who are leading.

Today, these emotions are promoted through various mechanisms and instruments, including businesses, governments, religions, marketing, media, news and film. We are bombarded daily with information that creates more and more collective emotions. Many people are manipulated through the creation of collective emotions. In fact, social marketing everywhere has as its basis the creation of collective emotions. Thus, collective emotions have become commodities of our market-driven society. It is clear that this is a premeditated strategy, so that we consume more, eat more, vote in a particular way... We live within an emotional culture. We live in an emotional economic culture. We live in an emotional political culture. We live within a social culture of emotions.

Those influences change our behavior and patterns of consumption. Suffice it to think of how many things we buy to achieve and maintain our "security". Let's not talk about armaments and other instruments where we spend trillions of dollars. This reality should make us reflect, and through that reflection, address a series of "ethical" questions.

Herewith some worrying attributes of collective emotions: an unpleasant experience; it invades everything in our life; it can remain forever; it creates a very "defensive" attitude of approaching life; in many cases, it paralyzes us; it prevents us from taking action; it is a modifier of our normal behavior; and it produces many unexpected behaviors and results; and it causes changes in ourselves, in human relationships, in relationships with nature; and collective emotions affect our body (health, through the nervous system) and our mind (anxiety, depression).

In addition to the above, there are important subtle attributes of emotions: collective emotions have life; and emotion is a living entity;

emotions organize and disorganize our life and habits; and as a living entity, it has a powerful "memory", which is present all the time; collective emotions show us the extremes.

Because these collective emotions are alive, they represent a state of being: they are an "internal state of being". Collective emotions mobilize us to act: to fight or to flee. They also mobilize us not to act: to be passive, paralyzed or disconnected.

Emotions are a form of energy. A special kind of energy. Most of the time, an inexhaustible form of energy. It never stops and keeps coming back. Its existence is almost permanent. The energy of emotions operates through the nervous system, affecting all other systems of our body.

Some questions arise: are there bad emotions and good emotions? Is there such a thing as "good emotion" and "bad emotion"? There are "good emotions: keeping our mind and soul awake (cautious, alert) and bad emotions (creates negative karma in ourselves and others).

Emotions are bad when they cut us off from our connection with the whole, with our origin, or with the unity. Therefore, even if we acquire a unique identity, we must never eliminate our connection with origin. This is a universal rule in all forms of consciousness. This also responds to a fundamental law of existence: it means returning to the experience of "perfection," the experience of the "present tense," and the experience of mindfulness.

Emotions are bad when they lead to behaviors and actions that ultimately create negative karmas. Also, referred to as "social emotions.

Different countries have different cultures of fear and experience different intensities of fear as a collective.

It is said that Germany is a country living in fear for decades. As a social phenomenon, fear is stronger in Germany than in many other European countries. Not long ago, there was an exhibition in Germany entitled: "Fear: a German state of mind".[25] Taking fear into account, the organizers chose themes that would be the "pain points" in fear: immigration, nuclear war, environmental destruction, and surveillance. Very interesting dimensions.

A similar situation is happening in the United States. Collective fear is a very common phenomenon. The US harbors a tremendous culture of fear. One of the most effective automatic triggers of collective fear is the news of a possible terrorist threat. Such a threat creates: vulnerability, sadness, anger and fear. This collective fear is the main source, for example, of a rupture in American identity and sense of belonging. This process of collective fear is accompanied by a series of emotions that are also shared collectively by the majority of citizens.

In relation to other countries, there are some classic and well-established emotions worth mentioning: the impacts of the invasion of another country (Crimea), the collective impacts that a "control of material wealth (land, water) has on people (the conflict between Chile and Bolivia). These causes of fear create a significant emotional response.

Collective fear is accompanied by the feeding of cultural symbols such as nationalist songs at street rallies, the use of flags and the intensification of other symbols that constitute strong sources of collective identity. Sometimes governments are not only very aware of these collective emotions, but also of the main causes (the origins of collective fears) of these collective emotions.

Because there are collective emotions, and they are alive, we have collective memory. It is through the memory, or the manipulation, of the facts contained in that collective memory, that emotions arise and transform our societies. The most basic attribute integrated into our collective memory (by what emerges as such) is the theme of "who we are within the collective".

As individuals, we are not an island, nor do we live in isolation. We are interdependent entities! The fact that we are interdependent brings several components or attributes that are constantly reverberating in the collective's memory.

Collective memory is also manipulated with reminders to keep our social memory alive, have to do with special names of streets, with advertising, the narrative in educational materials, and a series of created traditions by the establishment. People in power continue to hammer the past upon us, with the specific goal of achieving a certain collective purpose or behavior.

From a spiritual point of view, in order to correct or fight against these created collective emotions, we must connect, or reconnect, the collective memory with a state of "pure collective consciousness". Consciousness that I have an individual identity and a collective identity at the same time. Awareness that the individual and the collective are totally interdependent. Not separate. Two spheres in constant interaction. This is what I call "Container Consciousness". It is the container consciousness that represents the bridge between the individual consciousness and the collective consciousness. It is the container consciousness that establishes the non-material (spiritual) nature of our collective existence and conduct. It is the container consciousness that gives rise to "social attention," a state of being that very few people have incorporated into their lives.

We can conclude that, on an individual level, we experience the "independent attribute" of the self. Thus, individual fear. However, at the collective level we experience the "interdependent attribute" of the self. Therefore, it is the attribute of "interdependence" that brings collective fear into our lives.

COLLECTIVE VALUES

The actions we take are the result of the decisions we make. The decisions we make are the result of the beliefs and values we embrace. Values are not words or things. They are states of being. As states of being, we must self-realize them.

Today, we are dominated by individualistic and materialistic values: competition, competitiveness, exclusion, etc. To heal the planet, we must heal the collective: human beings, sentient beings and natural beings. To heal the planet, we must heal the collective: human beings, sentient beings and nature. To heal the collective, we must self-realize the collective values: love, compassion, solidarity, justice, cooperation, interdependence, etc. The self-realization of collective values is the positive and necessary energy for the healing of the planet.

BUDDHIST TEACHINGS ON LEADERSHIP AND COLLECTIVE EMOTIONS

Faced with different forms of emotion, the Buddha offers a number of possibilities: internal management of our path to the state of enlightenment. The Buddhist path has an individual and a collective dimension. As often expressed, the collective means the inclusion of all sentient beings. This is a big difference with other professionals dedicated to the understanding of collective emotions. In Buddhism, the approach is not to create a "war" with other people, or to create different forms of emotions. It is exactly the opposite. The path to an adequate social structure is achieved through peace.

This section is based on the teachings of the Buddha as described in at least three Sutras:

- *The Suda Abhaya Sutta*
- *The Anutanasati Sutta*

- *The Bhaya-Bherava Sutta*
- *The Satipatthana Sutta*
- *The Upajjhatthana Sutta*

The first teaching: the importance of the state of your karma.

The Buddha stated that there is a central connection between emotions (fear) and what you have done in your life. This teaching has to do with the formation of "merits" in our lives. The Buddha said that if you are in a good position (law of karma, without attachment) you will never have bad emotions. The reason is that being in a good position, they will feel satisfied, happy and content. This satisfaction, happiness and satisfaction will dissipate everything. If your life has not been right (too much negative karma, full of attachments, impurities), you will be full of emotions. That is why his advice was, among other things, to be pure in bodily conduct, pure in verbal conduct and pure in mental conduct.

The second teaching: knowledge and meditative experience.

In addressing emotions, the Buddha affirms that ignorance is the best way to strengthen your emotions.

The third teaching: the self-realization of forgiveness, detachment and the expansion of your own divinity.

Within the recommended practices, such as meditation, mindfulness, concentration, etc., become your own master. In addition, the Buddha recommends the practice of love and kindness.

The fourth teaching: Kriya Yoga. Here the Buddha teaches how to achieve mindfulness through the use of breathing.

And, through breathing and mindfulness, address your emotions. He states that, when practicing different ways of breathing, the important thing is to be in a state of observation. You are the observer and not the victim. You are an observer, not a judge. Being the observer is a very important concept, as fear invariably places you within the domain of the discriminating mind. We must be able to access our neutral mind.

The fifth teaching: to reach the state of the Buddha nature.

This state recognizes that "enlightenment" is a natural and true state of mind for all. In this context, if we want to get rid of negative emotions, we would need a different view of the practice of spirituality. In essence, Buddhist spirituality understands that our process of inner development must always be oriented towards the welfare of others. The Buddha of others. The Buddha affirms that all of us have the possibility of attaining an enlightened mind. A Buddha's mind. It is a universal characteristic of the human mind.

The sixth teaching: the power of awareness and concentration.

The Buddha affirms that emotions are stealing your mind. Concerns and demands imposed by emotions keep the mind in a permanent and distracted position. To stop this process, the Buddha's greatest teaching is the practice of concentration. Others have translated from Pali the term "concentration" as the practice of "full consciousness. Others, such as the practice of "mindfulness. Most of Buddha's teachings refer to concentration. Concentration will bring wisdom. And wisdom will defeat negative emotions.

The seventh teaching: to reach the 4 Jhana.

The Jhanas are states of consciousness. The first Jhana is a state of consciousness in which one attains isolation from sensual pleasures. The second Jhana is the consciousness in which we gain confidence in ourselves. The third Jhana is the consciousness that realizes equanimity, full attention and full consciousness. The fourth

Jhana is the consciousness that allows us to abandon pleasure and pain, and allows the disappearance of joy and pain.

The eighth teaching: achieving your dharma -your mission on this planet.

The Buddha declared that a person who is fulfilling his Dharma will be completely devoid of negative emotions. We have to practice love and kindness as an antidote. Your relationships will change drastically.

The ninth teaching: the practice of virtues controls all kinds of emotions.

The practice of compassion, loving kindness, equanimity, and joy. These virtues are the great eliminators of negative emotions. This is Karma Yoga.

The essence of Buddhist teachings is to transform the emotions of the leader into a transformation -inner and outer transformation— which will lead to 'spiritual awakening'.

No to stay in an illusory state or to maintain samsaric cycles (to repeat the problems of the past, meaningless cycles of life). Spiritual awakening means new energy and new consciousness for the leader. Spiritual awakening avoids that emotions keep us alienated to an unsuccessful past. This whole process is called "Samvega and Past". "Past" refers to this new energy. All of this is essential to leaders, so that they may defeat hopelessness, and the samsaric states at the individual and collective levels.

The Buddha recommended cultivating these emotions daily. Realizing and creating a new future and a new paradigm. Creating a future as a result of a sense of urgency. With a clear and serene confidence, which allows us to get out of "it". Also, develop noble qualities. All, based on the inner power of each one of us. This way we will be in the world without the world catching us.

EMOTIONS AFFECT ALL FORMS OF LIFE ON THE PLANET

For some people, we live in a society driven by collective emotions. Directing our society through collective emotions requires great leadership and material resources. Several sectors are flourishing because of collective emotions about the future of the planet. There is a tremendous fear among children and young people about global climate change, ozone depletion, biodiversity depletion, pollution of oceans and rivers, and more.

A new global strategy has to emerge. For it to emerge, we need a new consciousness. The old consciousness that has been used so effectively to fuel fear does not possess the attributes to eliminate fear. In fact, it is possible to change the world and transform the collective through the right type of leadership. Let us begin with an improvement of our purpose in life. Let us learn to face a new future. A new economy, a new politics and a new social paradigm must emerge. And this has to be the commitment of conscious leaders. The 21st Century needs a new form of leadership. It needs leaders with higher levels of consciousness.

CHAPTER XV:
THE SPIRITUAL FORMATION OF LEADERS

"Wise men talk because they have something to say; fools, because they have to say something." **— Plato**

"Those who are open-eyed are open-minded; those who are open-minded are open-hearted." **— Lao Tzu**

"You can never have an impact on society if you have not changed yourself." **— Nelson Mandela**

"Justice is a temporary thing that must at last come to an end; but the conscience is eternal and will never die." **— Martin Luther**

Leaders do not respond, or behave, by external stimulus only. The external environment is indeed important; however, leaders also respond to inner stimulus and inner growth and transformation.

The state of the soul, determines to a great extent the whole state of a leader. This state of the soul includes, for example: consciousness, awareness, concentration, wisdom, experience, absorptive capacity, ability to resolve, and skills to predict the future. This state of the soul is the real mechanism through which the leader captures, senses, conceptualizes situations and challenges, filters and determines the nature and scope of the vision of a leader, the nature of the external environment, and the capacity to lead others.

Thus, the importance of paying specific attention to the "non-material conditions" for decision-making in the unfolding of a true leader. This is what we call the spiritual dimension of leaders and leadership.

But this understanding goes far beyond human motivation and behavior per-se. It also shapes the leader's proposals for governance—individual and collective governance. Governance is understood as a live process of deliberation, participation, and exchange in making decisions. Governance is also understood as the institutional mechanism to create a critical path towards the shaping of a new future.

MULTIPLE INTELLIGENCE LEADERS

Governance as the practice of conscious sustainability leadership requires multiple intelligences. More and more we see how corporate leaders require a high level of emotional intelligence for their effective performance. They often face crises and difficulties that require not only emotional intelligence as ability to read their own and contextual emotions (EQ). They are expected to also read complex realities going from understanding and interpreting multifaceted organizations, systems and realities (IQ). They are expected to intelligently relate with diverse social and cultural contexts (CQ). They are expected to lead with moral intelligence based on principled actions and right intentions (MQ). These four-directions of the multiple intelligences expected from a leader are to be integrated in the leader's responsibility to carry on with re-imagining the idealistic vision synchronized to his/her calling (VQ) which needs to be articulated with proper plans and strategies through practical intelligence (PQ). Native American traditions have been pioneering the relevance of directions as interacting values and dimensions and have used the symbolic image of the turtle or tortoise in its four legs and four directions. The turtle for native populations of the oceans and tortoise for in land native population is considered a sacred animal for its shell and its ability to be in touch with its inner self symbolizing spiritual intelligence (SQ).

Spiritual and Multiple Intelligences

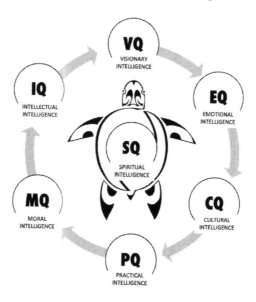

Figure 18: The Spiritual Direction at the Core of Leadership

Within this context of spiritual intelligence and spiritual directions, we should be aware of the fact that there are several ancient texts, some are Buddhist texts, which are extremely rich in suggesting attributes of a true spiritual leader.[26]

The Anatomy of a Buddhist Leader: Awakening the Leader from Within

It is important to share also the attributes of a leader, and one dimension of leadership, based on the "*Dassa Rajashama Buddhist Text*". In a conversation with a king, the Buddha refers to the following attributes, which are essential to address sustainability as defined here in this document.

The anatomy of a leader considers 10 key attributes: Generosity (Dana), Morality (Sila), Self-sacrifice (Pariccoga), Integrity (Ajjava), Kindness (Maddavam), Austerity (Tapa), Non-anger (Akkodha), Non-violence (Avihimsa), Tolerance (Khandhi), and Non-Deviation from Righteousness (Avirodama). It is not the objective here to write about each and every attribute; this goes beyond the scope of this chapter. However, it is important to note that there are several teachings of the Buddha that define, explain and indicate the way to the self-realization of each of these attributes.

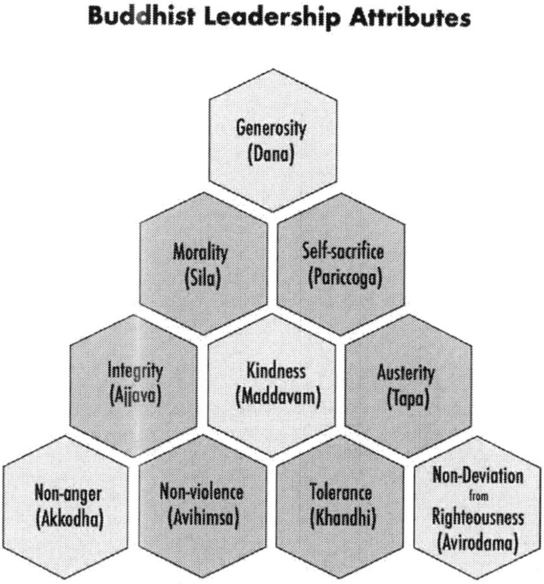

Buddhist Leadership Attributes

Figure 19: Buddhist Key Attributes of Leadership

The practice of Dana (generosity).

This means to share with others in a beneficial way objects that would improve other beings' material and spiritual welfare. It also may mean forgiveness as an act of generosity. In addition, generosity may also include the giving of the right advice to all living beings.

The practice of Sila (morality, moral standing).

This means, for example, maintaining good conduct and behavior so that the leader and followers do not breach ethical principles and morals (it may include religious and spiritual morals, laws and ethical norms (individual and social norms). Practical ways that are very essential in addressing sustainability in development are: not to harm living beings, not to steal or gain from misappropriation, not to create intoxication (pesticides, herbicides, agrochemicals), etc. Because it addresses morals, the ancient texts also include areas of a leader's behavior having to do with sexual misconduct and lying. Not lying is essential when governments of corporations withhold essential information regarding pollution, quality of food ingredients (e.g., addictive substances), and the like.

The practice of Pariccoga (selfless sacrifice for the greater good).

This means that the leader embodies an inner concern and preoccupation about the prosperity of others. This is often called a concern about "greater prosperity", including also the wealth of communities and cities, or any other human settlement. Today, the greater prosperity includes the whole planet, all sentient beings and the future generations to come. This understanding would result in the leader's own determination to establish institutions of universal learning.

The practice of Ajjava (integrity).

This integrity will include, for example, a great sense of loyalty, the courage to bring a great sense of truthfulness, and a constant search for honesty. The admission of the truth is an important part of this path. This is also a path of perseverance and honesty, and the honoring of promises (a good attribute when one debates the contribution of individual countries to the attainment of the SDGs).

The practice of Maddavan (kindness).

The leaders must be gentle and open-minded, as opposed to being egocentric and arrogant. This is an attribute that heightens the importance of the right behavior and interaction with others. The leader, being in a privileged position, must show that all the forms of interactions with others are done in the correct way: sincerity, peaceful, gentle, etc.

The practice of Tapa (austerity).

The leader is expected to have a simple life, and not a life of indulgence (material indulgence) and various sensual pleasures. Today, there is a need to defeat the hypothesis that "more is better'; a principle, which has been responsible for the over exploitation of our natural resources and environmental services. In our societies, there is no incentive for "less" and understanding frugality in its various expressions. The new leaders must change that. It has been said also that the leader should be diligent in consistently performing the important duties.

The practice of Akkodha (non-anger).

The leader's inner existence must not show anger, hate, or vindictiveness against others. Compassion (karouna) is one essential attribute of the new leader. In this case, 'karouna' means: "to have an ability to become the other without losing one's own identity. In many ways, the expression "non-anger" means that the leader lives outside the domain of anger; both, in the relative and in the absolute.

The practice of Avihimsa (non-violence).

The leader must not inflict harm on others including animals and all living things, adhering to peace and tranquility for all and not indulging himself in his power. By not inflicting harm on anyone and instead decide to establish the forms of practical learning that will benefit all.

The practice of Khandi (tolerance).

The leader must be patient and be capable of addressing all types of emotions, be they greed, anger, ignorance or any kind of suffering. The leader must not use abrasive words and maintain calmness in his mind, composure in his daily behavior, and care deeply about the body and words. It is essential to be patient with the ignorance of his subjects at all levels.

The practice of Avirodhana (righteousness).

The leader must not allow misdeeds, and should be just. This issue of justice is particularly relevant as regards the management of natural resources and the environment between and among generations. This is often referred to today as Environmental Justice or Climate Justice. Righteousness also includes the fight against ignorance so that the leadership qualities are not confused with orders or traditional disciplinary actions.

LEADERSHIP AS THE ROAD TO AVOID AND ELIMINATE SUFFERING

As we all know, one essential foundation of Buddhism is to avoid suffering. Thus, one could postulate that in a significant way, leadership must become a unique and effective way so that every being on the planet is able to avoid suffering. This was the first and most powerful of all Buddha's teachings: "The Four Noble Truths" and "The 8-Fold Path."

All of the above raises several questions which are directly linked with the CSL paradigm proposed here. These questions also serve to address a large number of business management practices one sees today in the corporate world. Examples of these questions are:

What is the role of spirituality in business?

For decades, most people see spirituality and business as oil and vinegar. They do not mix. The fact that businesses are guided by money and profits leaves no room to think or address non-material dimensions of business; e.g., love, compassion, solidarity, cooperation, inclusion, equity, justice, interdependence, and more. This has radically changed during the last couple of decades. Not only we see a change in the way human resource development is addressed but also how a given business takes care of its impacts on the outer environment surrounding the business. This is the case of the impacts of business practices on sustainable development, environment and ecology (natural and human ecology), at the national and global levels. The role of spirituality is also important in deciding about alternative forms of business management.

What are the ethical, human, and moral responsibilities of business?

Recently, business owners and managers are being asked about ethics and moral issues. Is it ethical to pollute a lake and to destroy biodiversity? In some ways, the whole notion of Social Corporate Responsibility touches on the fact that these responsibilities could be both material and non-material, they could be related to production processes as well as impacts on the life of consumers and their local environment. This is also relevant in the discussion of consumer safety regarding food and nutrition, the use of agrochemicals and GMO seeds, the contamination of air and water, the accelerated depletion of natural resources, and the like. Issues of natural resources management are now central to the operation of all business.

Is there a better definition of Corporate Social Responsibility (CSR), or is this notion another communication myth?

This question is relevant because CSR is not just about philanthropy. It is not just a voluntary mechanism to increase the positive impacts of business on people and the natural environment. It is a true social responsibility. This is to say that business should not only produce clean and safe products, for example, but they should commit to a society that is clean and safe. There is a clear social dimension. Also, beyond voluntarism, CSR is a collection of very concrete decisions, policies, programs and projects, which have to be launched to drive towards the desired results. It is as concrete as something can be, but its conceptual origin is non-material in nature: "social responsibility".

Why do managers and staff see business and spirituality as two separate/opposite dimensions of human life?

Many managers see spirituality and business as two separate entities, spaces to operate into, and attributes of daily life. This is a duality that has permeated many business practices and activities. This is a duality also ingrained within those corporate owners and managers. This is a duality that, when it exists, it will show in every aspect and dimension of those corporate actors: at home (treating family members well but employees not so well), in the neighborhood (creating many barriers to the entry of lower income groups: "us" here vs. "them" there), in religion (my religion is the best compared to others), in politics, etc. Business and spirituality are not two separate dimensions of human life. They are one and the same, and it is time to bring spirituality into business now.

What are the non-material responsibilities of business in this new millennium?

This is not an esoteric question. The world is facing tremendous challenges like climate change, biodiversity depletion, pollution of the oceans, the degeneration of glaciers, the rapid loss of quality of life, and the like. Business bears a great responsibility for the management of these global public goods. It is not only the responsibility of government or public authorities. Without the engagement of the private sector, no real progress will be attained towards a sustainable society. Another non-material responsibility is the protection of the planet, for the enjoyment of future generations. Again, this is not just voluntary; it demands specific actions today in order to create a new future. The new leaders must be ready to tackle these non-material responsibilities.

How to move out of old patterns and inadequate styles of management?

Corporate actions are often translated via different styles of management. Including both: the management of the corporation itself as well as the management of its external impact on the social and environmental dimensions. As presented in this book, there are very questionable styles of management, like management by fear or terror. One may increase productivity, but this productivity is gained at the expense of the human factor. At the expense of workers and of all who work for the corporation. The conscious leader must be equipped to address not only the hardware, but also the software of corporate development and transformation. This is imperative as we move into the next industrial revolution, also another theme of this book.

What are the most effective instruments and techniques to change the managers' levels of awareness/consciousness and become more effective in all dimensions of business?

The manager, the leader, and all of those involved within the corporate world must be given the instruments and mechanisms to expand their consciousness, deepen their experiences and be able to lead in a desirable world, for the corporation and or all the corporation touches. There is not a conscious corporation without a conscious leader(s). This statement may sound trivial, but as we know nothing is trivial when it comes to the expansion of corporate consciousness. This suggests a major change in corporate planning and implementation, for the medium and long term, where new spaces for inner development of leaders and managers is urgently required.

How would corporations move from Business Entrepreneurship (BuE) to Social Entrepreneurship (SoE), and from Social Entrepreneurship to Spiritual Entrepreneurship (SpE)?

Corporate development and enterprise growth and transformation are not separate from alternative forms of entrepreneurship. In our view, there is a virtuous cycle of entrepreneurship, starting with business entrepreneurship: being conscious or aware of the needs and challenges of a corporation as a business. One example is that of the creation of a barcode to register different products. The entrepreneur is conscious of the business. The next step is social entrepreneurship, when the entrepreneur is not only aware of the impacts on business but also on the external impacts the business creates as it develops. This is the outer consciousness and aware of business. Finally, this virtuous cycle not only includes awareness of the business and its external impact, but also the entrepreneur must be aware of his or herself. This inner awareness conditions the outer awareness and the business awareness. It is the inner awareness that sets the limits of leadership.

What is the meaning of a self-realized leader as different from a knowledgeable or competent leader?

Most business practices, and the academic work that accompanies it, are an outcome of the relationship between "knowledge" and "action": to know and to do. Where a lot of attention is put into expanding knowledge to improve decisions and actions. However, now, we are not in the era of knowledge but in the era of wisdom. Thus, action must be fully linked with the leader self-realization process: "so I self-realize, so I act". The golden rule of leadership has dramatically changed. It is not about knowledge per-se, it is not about age, it is not about diplomas...it is about wisdom. This is a quantum change in the improvement of leadership around the world. We must be self-realized leaders.

How have business strategies and aims evolved during the last few years at the corporate level? (e.g., incorporation of human rights and corresponding implications).

Everything in business, formally or informally, touches the edges or the heart of corporate strategies and aims, as they set the scene for all forms of business activities. These aims and strategies must be constantly evolving. Thus, leadership must be constantly evolving to address sustainable development, human rights, corporate responsibility, the management of global public goods, and much more. To move from quantity to quality, from extraction to conservation, from time bound decision to instantaneous decisions, from markets to citizens, etc.

When and how do we need to form the leader of the future? (Who will be the next superpower)?

Leadership is not only about individual leadership, or corporate leadership. It is also about planetary leadership, collective leadership. The aggregation of leadership towards a world view that embraces all the nations of the world. Leadership at that level is changing, from USA supremacy to many other alternatives. These are not only described as economic based, but also it incorporates culture, values, interdependence, etc. Thus, we see the possibilities of China, Russia, India, Brazil, and some other European countries. It is vital to acquire the notion of country conscious leadership, going far beyond economic leadership.

The ancient texts also recognized that one obligation of the conscious leader was to protect animals and the environment, provide for the poor, and avoid greed, and taking that to which one is not entitled.

The path to leadership also considers a number of efforts the leader should engage into: knowing the causes and conditions; knowing the real purpose of leading; knowing oneself; knowing the right time (timing); knowing the group or the society that is leading, knowing the path towards the self-realization of harmony (with other human beings, with sentient beings, and nature), and knowing that nobody has the right to destroy nature and life.

BOX 4: ASADHAMMA SUTTA - DISCOURSE ON THE TEN DHAMMAS

"Thus, have I heard:

On one occasion the Blessed One was living near Savatthi at Jetavana at the Monastery of Anathapindika.

Then the Blessed One addressed the monks, saying: "Monks." — "Venerable Sir," they said by way of reply. The Blessed One then spoke as follows:

"These ten essentials (Dhammas) must be reflected upon again and again by one who has gone forth (to live the holy life). What are these ten?"

1. "'I am now changed into a different mode of life (from that of a layman).' This must be reflected upon again and again by one who has gone forth.

2. "'My life depends on others.' this must be reflected upon again and again by one who has gone forth.

3. "'I must now behave in a different manner.' This must be reflected upon again and again by one who has gone forth.

4. "'Does my mind upbraid me regarding the state of my virtue?' (Sila). This must be reflected upon again and again by one who has gone forth.

5. "'Do my discerning fellow-monks having tested me, reproach me regarding the state of my virtue?' This must be reflected upon again and again by one who has gone forth.

6. "'There will be a parting (someday) from all those who are dear and loving to me. Death brings this separation to me.' This must be reflected upon again and again by one who has gone forth.

7. "'Of kamma (Literally action — mental, verbal, and physical) I am constituted. Kamma is my inheritance; kamma is the matrix; kamma is my kinsman; kamma is my refuge. Whatever kamma I perform, be it good or bad, to that I shall be heir.' This must be reflected upon again and again by one who has gone forth.

8. "'How do I spend my nights and days?' This must be reflected upon again and again by one who has gone forth.

9. "'Do I take delight in solitude?' This must be reflected upon again and again by one who has gone forth.

10. "'Have I gained superhuman faculties? Have I gained that higher wisdom so that when I am questioned (on this point) by fellow-monks at the last moment (when death is approaching) I will have no occasion to be depressed and downcast?' This must be reflected upon again and again by one who has gone forth.

"These, monks, are the essentials that should be reflected again and again by one who has gone forth (to live the holy life)."

So spoke the Blessed One.

Those monks rejoiced at the words of the Blessed One."[27]

CHAPTER XVI:
FUNDAMENTALS OF LEADERSHIP

"The central, most telling question to ask a leader is, whom do you serve? Asking the question whom do you serve? is a powerful vector on which to build a useful typology of six levels of leadership: Sociopath, Opportunist, Chameleon, Achiever, Builder, and Transcendent. Level-six leaders transcend their political party, their ethnic or racial group, and even their institutions. They focus on how to benefit all of society. These are "global citizens."

— Mitch Maidique

"A leader is best when people barely know he exists. When his work is done, his aim fulfilled, they will say: we did it ourselves."

— Lao Tzu

"The two most important days in your life are the day you are born and the day you find out why."

—Mark Twain

To enter into the space of leadership is a rather complex matter. One would have to cover immense space to do justice to the present debate. Thus, several theoretical and paradigmatic aspects of existing approaches will not be treated comprehensively here. The main attention will be on the SL paradigm.

SOME BASIC DEFINITIONS

The term 'leadership' has been used and abused. All sorts of definitions are being put forth to the general public, even to say that leadership is a form of good governance. It is as if leadership can be anything and contain everything.

We have rescued a few definitions for the layperson and for a rapid understanding of what we are talking about. One, leadership as a process to lead, guide and influence the behavior and actions of others in relationship to objectives and goals. Two, leadership as the opportunity to influence behavior of others, via new visions, intentions and language. Like a form of real persuasion in the core of the human factor.

For the most functional minds, leadership is an important factor of production, and as such most leadership models have followed the incentives and the laws of the market. This is why we see how corporate leadership focuses so much on competitiveness, productivity, organizational change, incentives to produce more, and consume more. This is a form of leadership where "more is better".

KEY LEADERSHIP THEORIES

In addition to the above, it is relevant at least to mention the most important leadership theories, with the understanding that this presentation only represents the tip of a huge iceberg. Herewith some of these theories.

The Evolution of Leadership Theories

Figure 20: The Leadership Theories Evolution

The experts say that there are too many leadership theories; however, most of them can be classified into eight significant groups:

First, the Great Man Theory, which says that the great leaders are born as a leader. Thus, the capacity to be a good leader is inherent to that person. A concept rooted in male energy.

Second, the Traits Theory, which focuses on attributes that seem to be characteristic of a leader. Thus, the attention on these attributes of leaders. Some have written a lot about the traits of 'effective leaders', and based on those, many generalizations are made. It is also said that a leader can be made and molded.

Third, the Contingency Theory, which pays attention to those aspects that are related to the environment where leadership is exercised. Thus, the environment is an intervening variable in shaping up different styles of leadership.

Fourth, the Situational Theory, which emphasizes the uniqueness of a situation; e.g., who knows best and exercising a more centralized form of leadership, or where the collective is more active, demanding a more even form of leadership.

Fifth, the Behavioral Theory, which is based upon the belief that leaders are made and not necessarily born. Thus, more focus on what the leader does (action oriented) than on its attributes.

Sixth, the Participative Theory, which advocates that a good style of leadership is nurtured by inputs from others (leaders and followers). This improves that relationship and creates more effective decision-making processes.

Seventh, the Business Management Theory, which we have addressed above, and that focuses on key corporate functions including performance, competitiveness, supervision, organizational structures... Because of the nature of business, leadership is often exercised by a series of incentives and 'carrots and sticks'.

Eighth, the Relationship Theory, which focuses strongly in understanding the relationships that exist between leaders and followers. This is a collective form of leadership. The key ingredients are inspiration, inspiration, and traction. Here, there is a notion of maximizing people's potential.

CONSCIOUS SUSTAINABILITY LEADERSHIP (CSL)

Herewith the essence of the CSL paradigm:

1. While this chapter intends to strengthen the SL paradigm, the totality of this chapter begins to suggest a new paradigm for

sustainability leadership: "Conscious Sustainability Leadership (CSL)". SL as stated now is of the same nature of the paradigm of management leadership, but to be applied in a different context.

2. CSL is, in essence, rooted into the inner transformation of leaders. Not only their outer experience, in the outer environment, but also their inner experience, in the inner environment. This confirms the importance of the inter-relationship between our inner ecology and our outer ecology. This awareness induces us to aspire to an enlightened form of leadership: awareness of the outer and of the inner.

3. CSL is not an individual state of reality. Actually, the individual aspects are only a small proportion of the total. The total contains a very important collective state of reality; a theme running through this entire proposal. Leadership is not only about the leader but also about the followers. It is a mutual state of existence.

4. CSL of the future cannot be a male-energy-based paradigm. It is imperative to understand leadership as a fruit of the feminine: feminine energy, feminine qualities of leaders, feminine foundations of leadership, the feminine perspectives and components of sustainable development, etc. It will be this feminine energy the one that will bring together our material and spiritual realities.

5. CSL is a form of leadership with no spatial or inter-temporal boundaries. The global extension of leadership includes not only geographical areas (the countries, the regions, and the planet), but it also draws down boundaries with regard to the key actors -human beings and all sentient beings—and with regard to its influence on the quality of life of future generations. Another key feature within the realm of leadership for sustainable development.

6. In writing this note, I am fully aware of the powerful influence of western culture on the leadership debate. Perhaps, too much. It is time we expand and embrace eastern philosophies and cultures and

enrich the debate on sustainability. Here, we have made some efforts to distill some of the contributions of a paradigm such as Buddhism. A whole book could be written about Buddhist Leadership.

7. Perhaps, the most important ingredient of the SL paradigm rests on the need to connect—time after time—the local and the global aspects of sustainability. Such effort is to be carried out understanding that while these are interconnected, they are completely different realities. Thus, the many famous phrases in our social grammar (e.g., "think globally, act locally"). This necessitates the creation of a global platform for leadership; today, non-existing. The global dimensions are not trivial to address: global awareness, global cooperation, global governance and institutions. A lot has been written on each and every aspect of these global aspects of leadership. In other words, global leadership is a composite of different ingredients.

8. Humanity is having to handle high levels of complexities. Just think about global warming and climate change. Everything must be included. All actors need to be involved. And, every aspect of our lives is to be modified and transformed. These are not marginal moves. These are deeply structural reforms. This complexity demands a new form of leadership. This complexity demands the expansion of human consciousness.

9. To set global strategic directions still remains in a weak foundation. To start with, few people have an understanding of the nature and scope of a world calculus and a world unit of account. To attain these aspects of leadership, one would need to propose a very strong paradigm on collective leadership. What is this collective leadership? What is good collective leadership?

10. The public-good nature and character of sustainability leadership versus other forms of leadership. Sustainability leadership embodies a form of public good, as it is address to publics goods proper (e.g., oceans, climate, ozone layer, biodiversity), but also, the

lack of sustainability leadership or its inadequate implementation creates various "public bads" (e.g., pollution, global warming, resource depletion, poverty, diseases). Its public good nature is a very unique feature of sustainability leadership.

The above is not all. The CSL involves also elements of Human leadership, Spiritual leadership, Conscious leadership, Values leadership, Love leadership, Ethical leadership, Moral leadership, Feminist leadership, Cultural leadership, Ethnic leadership, Wholeness leadership, Ecological leadership, and Organizational leadership.

Leadership Elements of CSL

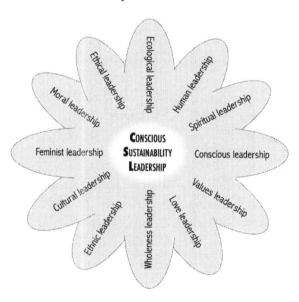

Figure 21: The Elements of CSL

In a society governed by citizens, a hierarchical concept of a leader has no meaning, particularly when the expectations are that leadership has to translate into empowerment. Because of this, some have suggested that worrying too much about who are true "leaders", and who are not, does not make much sense.

Finally, we would like to point out how weak is the literature on sustainability leadership, by saying that sustainable development is not the topping of the cake, or the jewel in the crown. It is the cake and it is the crown. It is all and, thus, the debate has to penetrate politics, economics, social change, poverty, foreign policy, creation of communities, creation of a conservation culture, creating a humanistic whole, moving towards caring economics, promoting other forms of values, creating a space for "ecofeminism".

We do not want to be critical, but most of them are very similar, and some of the debates are devoted to splitting hairs. Today, we do not even distinguish well between sustainability leadership and ecological/environmental leadership. It is evident that these are not the same; but writers tend to put everything in one bag.

It is clear to me that in the future we will have to define whether SL is an attribute or a philosophy, a core value or a value system, a state of awareness, etc. The role of neurosciences and quantum leadership models are to be taken into account.

In the corporate world, much attention should be paid to how one systematically brings sustainability concerns into the core of a business model, and how one recognizes the importance of sustainability as a factor to organizational transformation.

LEADERSHIP, JUSTICE AND RIGHTS

We live in a society where rights are central responsibilities to the attainment of objectives and goals of development. These are not just Civil and Political Rights, though extremely relevant, particularly on debates about the rights to life and the rights to a decent and clean environment. In fact, we agree with those who have proposed that leadership and sustainable development acquire a new meaning within what is called "The Right Based Approach to Development". This is an approach not based on the market and the excessive translations into commodities and values. For example, education is not a commodity, it is a right and, thus, it is not to be implemented guided by a profit-making criterion. People have the right to free education.

The key concern here is with the rights of sentient beings and nature. We know that some countries, like Ecuador, have already declared the rights to nature; a crucial outcome of sustainability leadership.

Concomitant to this is the whole process of empowerment of citizens, everywhere. Most people want to be part of the change proposed here. This proposal changes completely the type of leadership one is to exercise within the human collective. Perhaps, this suggests major reforms, including those reforms that would lead to a very different process of industrialization. A new revolution where the critical path we have to walk through is from steam engines to the highest levels of human consciousness. This is when leadership becomes central to the formation and strengthening of communities.

It is impossible to even start a debate on sustainability leadership without including the development paradigm advocated by indigenous peoples, women, youth and senior citizens. All, have powerful visions that are to be considered, and integrated into the whole debate on the formation of leaders and leadership. These are powerful examples of how the social and environmental concerns go hand in hand.

Finally, nothing of leadership at the collective level will be implemented without political commitment. This opens a huge debate on the linkages between sustainability leadership and political

leadership. Can one go against the other? A big dilemma today.
This raises even more questions regarding leadership at the collective
level.

BOX 5: COMMON LEADERSHIP STYLES AND THEORIES

Here are some leadership theories which also reflect what we have observed first
hand in our professional experiences. These brief summaries can help us reflect
on our own preferred style in relation to our call for leadership and sustainability
and perhaps consider a different leadership style if a new leadership approach is
needed to address the needs of your organization.[28]

Visionary (Systemic) Leadership: This type of leadership reflects
characteristics of leadership that should be common in everyone but certain
leaders simply excel at this. Systems thinking is an essential mind-set and skill-
set for today's leaders who aspire to make social impact and sustainable
development changes. The leader is expected to know political, economic, social,
cultural and other systems affected and effecting change. The advantage of this
visionary / systemic leadership style is the ability to engage and communicate an
idea in an enthusiastic and vibrant way with a variety of stakeholders. The
disadvantage of this leadership style is that it requires the leader to engage
beyond their own sector and immediate level of expertise. The visionary /
systemic leader style finds a good fit with someone leading a new initiative or the
drama of changing contexts.

Entrepreneur (Charismatic) Leadership: This type of leadership presents
characteristics of a founder and someone who is able to begin, design and
implement projects, organization and initiatives that inspire others. The leader is
expected to convey an engaging message to shareholders and stakeholders and
the followers who are expected to trust the charismatic proposition. The
advantage of entrepreneur / charismatic leadership style is to promote socially
and sustainability beneficial innovations. The disadvantage is that the initiatives
may not be scalable and impactful in the long-run and the leader may not be able
to lead the initiative into more mature levels of its created organizations /

institutions. Entrepreneur / charismatic leaders are valued in innovative and change-seeking situations.

Delegating (Laissez-Faire) Leadership: This type of leadership is the opposite of autocratic leadership. This style works well with well trained and experienced employees who do not require much supervision or interference from the leader to accomplish their work. The advantage of this style of leadership is that it provides an opportunity for the employees / followers to be creative in their work as well as grow as leaders themselves. The disadvantage is that when there is a need for directions the established routine of non-interference may be hard to change. Delegating / laissez-faire leaders are most effective when the organization / initiative is mature enough to share its sense of ownership and responsibility.

Autocratic (Authoritarian) Leadership: This type of leadership is the opposite of delegating leadership. It is the style of someone who is focused almost entirely on results and efficiency. The leader is expected to know the know what needs to be done and the follower is expected to follow the commands without question. The advantage of this is to be able to lead people and organizations in times of crisis and emergencies when prompt decisions need to be made firmly and immediately. The disadvantage is that it discourages or impedes workers / followers' creativity and innovation. The autocratic / authoritarian leaders are much appreciated in times of emergency and in high power-distance cultures. This type of leadership style stunts a productive work environment for many workers.

Participative (Democratic) Leadership: This type of leadership presents a balance between the autocratic (controlling) and the delegating (laissez-faire). It works well in engaged workplaces and organizations desiring innovation. The leader is expected to seek the inputs and the follower is expected to actively contribute to the decision-making process. The advantage of participative leadership is that followers are engaged as they feel they are making a significant contribution. The disadvantage is that it may slow down the processes when decisions need to be made quickly or when followers are unprepared or uninformed. The participative / democratic leaders are much appreciated in participatory processes of decision making and in low-power distance cultures.

Coaching (Mentoring) Leadership: This type of leadership is of someone who can easily recognize the workers / followers' values, strengths, weaknesses and motivations to set smart goals and give feedback to encourage growth. The leader is expected to be a good listener and the followers are expected to own their own leadership development journey. The advantage of this coaching leadership style is that it creates a positive and motivating environment. The disadvantage is that, unfortunately, this is an underutilized style because it can be time-intensive. The coaching / mentoring leaders are much appreciated when educational and personal growth are priorities in organizations and in more individualistic cultures.

Performance (Pacesetter) Leadership: This type of leadership style is usually helpful in later stages of organizational developments when the primary concern is productivity and efficiency. The leader is expected to know the production process well and set clear expectations with targeted goals and indicators for measuring performance and the followers should be competent managers and workers who know how to deliver. The advantage of the performance / pacesetter leadership style is to elevate the organization / initiative into a high level of productivity, scalability and impact. The disadvantage is that it may make short-sighted decisions while privileging opportunistic partnerships and fostering sterile relations. The performance / pacesetter leaders are much appreciated in scalable initiatives, growing organizations, and where the cultural values are more on profit, productivity and performance.

Adaptive (Situational) Leadership: This type of leadership style is capable of adapting diverse responses and relations based on the situation. The leader is expected to understated the organizational needs, the political opportunities and cultural contexts and the followers are expected to accept the different treatment and standards across the organization and individuals. The advantage of the adaptive / situational leadership style is that the same leader could be the right person for diverse organizational stages, worker's needs and sector's constituencies. The disadvantage is that a jack-of-all-trades person may not be able to project authenticity and integrity. The adaptive / situational leaders are appreciated in ever changing and diverse eco-systems where specific situations need well thought out and diverse responses.

Bureaucratic (Transactional) Leadership: These types of leaders exemplify similar characteristics in their concern for following rules and procedures precisely. Following the contract and not-violating policies are more important than productivity and innovation. Usually predetermined monetary incentives or punishment mechanisms are used to enforce the agreements. Leaders are expected to stick to the rules and followers are expected to follow policies and their contracts. The advantage of bureaucratic / transactional leadership styles is that they are more effective in highly regulated industries or departments, such as finance, healthcare or government. The disadvantage is that it inhibits engagement and discourages creativity and innovation. The bureaucratic / transactional leaders are appreciated when there is a need for justice, accountability and transparency.

Servant (Transformational) Leadership: The servant and transformational leadership styles are similar and we combine them here as they exhibit a similar attention to the common mission and aligned motivations of leaders / followers. The leader is expected to operate beyond self-interests and totally dedicated to the cause while followers are willing to engage beyond contractual or monetary rewards. The advantage of the servant / transformational leadership styles is that it engages the follower's individual goals into the organization's common cause and mission. The disadvantage is that these leaders may place importance on the big picture without the ability to manage critical individual needs and important operational details. The servant / transformational leaders are appreciated in high-purpose organizations and cultures who value the common good.

CHAPTER XVII:
A CASE OF WRONG LEADERSHIP

"People will do anything, no matter how absurd, in order to avoid facing their own souls. One does not become enlightened by imagining figures of light, but by making the darkness conscious."–**Carl Jung**

"On some positions, Cowardice asks the question, "Is it safe?" Expediency asks the question, "Is it politic?" And Vanity comes along and asks the question, "Is it popular?" But Conscience asks the question "Is it right?" And there comes a time when one must take a position that is neither safe, nor politic, nor popular, but he must do it because Conscience tells him it is right."–**Martin Luther King, Jr.**

"In our consciousness, there are many negative seeds and also many positive seeds. The practice is to avoid watering the negative seeds, and to identify and water the positive seeds every day."–**Thich Nhat Hanh**

"My conscience hath a thousand several tongues, and every tongue brings in a several tales, and every tale condemns me for a villain."–**William Shakespeare, Richard III**

OVERVIEW

Most articles about management are written for managers. However, it is important and timely to write about management from the perspective of those who are managed and subject to limitless experiments, practices and working conditions produced by the regular changes in fashion in management theories and styles.

Corporations readily bring their clients' perspectives into their ethos and management styles. As they respond to client demands via organizational fine-tuning, it is also crucial that they take a look at management from the point of view and experiences of their employees. Unfortunately, most managers do not see the people whom they manage as clients, though in many ways they should. Instead, they often consider their staff as instruments to reach those whom they see as the true (i.e., external) clients for their products and services.

Every time a company introduces a new management style, it subjects its managers and managers-to-be to intense training. This trend continues widely, despite the fact that many managers report that the training has limited impacts on their everyday lives. Most managers know that more training is not tantamount to enhanced managerial ability, and many courses have little to do with being or becoming a better manager. Moreover, no significant correlation has been found between improvements in managers' quality of life and more training, promotions or higher pay. It is the exception rather than the rule.

In many ways, the standard approach to management training – e.g., behavioral modification-- has not been successful because its outcomes have frequently not been sustainable. Therefore, those who ask themselves whether taking additional training or qualifying for new forms of certification will lead to higher managerial positions should think twice about it.

In my (Alfredo) corporate experience, the best managers were simply those who trusted their staff, cared about them as persons, listened to them and were willing to seriously consider their advice. This management style, which I'll call "management by trust" (MBTrust), invariably brings an inner force and commitment to the management process that cannot be compared to anything else.

People do not like to work with supervisors who don't trust them. An atmosphere of mistrust can arise as a result of many factors. For example, mistrust can result from a manager's belief that he/she is the best, and thus, the staff can never perform assignments to the manager's standards. Managers also generate mistrust by setting impossible or unrealistic targets for their staff.

Today, we find hundreds of books promoting different management approaches, methods and practices; however, behavioral modification theory underlies a large number of their recommendations. However, the instruments and techniques suggested by behavioral modification theory seem to work wonders only when managers have a strong, post-training support system. Without this, whatever has been learned tends to vanish rather quickly.

Time and again, major behavioral changes revert to old management practices in the absence of this proper support system. After the training, managers go back to the office full of brio, with good knowledge and a strong desire to improve themselves. However, when they find that they have to fight the same old battles again and again, they most often abandon the new tools and practices received during training.

The focus on management training is at a high. Personnel manuals and directives are rapidly multiplying and are now often much larger than operational manuals. Personnel departments are growing by leaps and bounds, as is their influence in the corporate world. Management consulting firms are becoming equally powerful and prosperous, as they regularly create new management models and dismantle old ones. At the moment, consultants widely recommend management by objectives and management for results, to make corporations more accountable in relation to their mandates, which is reasonable.

However, I have observed that the determinants for effective management remain obscure for most people. In addition, the height of the bar that gauges managerial success is constantly changing, and it is doing so right now. As management theories shift in popularity, companies undergo excessive and often unnecessary structural changes that deeply affect career development and personal stability. All this creates great uncertainty in the minds of the managed.

In the end, some fundamental questions remain: Does a clear, proven relationship exist between productivity and a high level of employee job satisfaction? Are the two interdependent or unrelated? If interdependent, are managers and their practices improving the lives of working people? Is this even an objective of training, or is the corporation bottom line the only consideration?

MANAGEMENT BY TERROR (MBTERROR)

The average employee may see many factors taken into consideration regarding promotion to management positions that have little or nothing to do with being a good manager. In some cases, promotion is even linked to a harsh management style. In fact, a number of corporations and governments, nationally and globally, use what may be called "management by terror" (MBTerror). Widely used in both private and public entities, MBTerror is currently very popular, though generally unacknowledged, approaches to management.

Management by terror promotes instruments and advocates corporate values that are principally related to fear: threats, violence, intimidation, exaggeration, destruction of self-confidence, excessive hierarchical relationships, creation of personal and collective anxiety and forced submission to a changing goal. It creates unpleasant experiences, artificial crises and constant worry. Obviously, these instruments and values are not always implemented in an overt or forthright manner. They are most often employed with subtlety and sophistication, and their implementation is often accompanied by a strong and comprehensive communication strategy and other means of legitimization.

MBTerror managers—we can call them corporate terrorists—show high levels of effectiveness within the very short-term, while failing and becoming unsustainable in the long term. The exception to this comes when the large majority of managers in a given corporation practice MBTerror, and thus the approach is legitimized across the board for a longer time.

MBTerror must be put into practice in elaborate ways, especially those that want to avoid lawsuits, retaliatory legal actions and formal counter-responses from unions, employee associations, etc. Therefore, one has to go beyond the surface and the regular connotation of some of the terms used to define MBTerror. Though MBTerror managers often get away with various unacceptable forms of behavior and practices, e.g., harassment, we should note the consequences of that behavior. For example, the psychological and physical stress regularly produced by MBTerror often costs corporations millions of dollars in health insurance claims, absenteeism, civil suits, etc.

Let us focus here only on a sample of elements embodied in MBTerror. If this allows the reader to understand this form of management better, he/she might then be able to cope and find the strong counter influences and instruments so much needed for a decent working life.[29] Some of the material presented here comes from private conversations, particularly with those who have been negatively affected by this form of management.

Dynamics of Managing by Terror

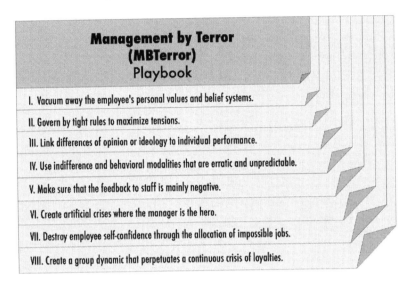

Management by Terror (MBTerror) Playbook

I. Vacuum away the employee's personal values and belief systems.

II. Govern by tight rules to maximize tensions.

III. Link differences of opinion or ideology to individual performance.

IV. Use indifference and behavioral modalities that are erratic and unpredictable.

V. Make sure that the feedback to staff is mainly negative.

VI. Create artificial crises where the manager is the hero.

VII. Destroy employee self-confidence through the allocation of impossible jobs.

VIII. Create a group dynamic that perpetuates a continuous crisis of loyalties.

Figure 22: The MBTerror Playbook

THE INSTRUMENTS OF TERROR

I. Vacuum away the employee's personal values and belief systems

Most courses in business management lead us to believe that management is value neutral. Certainly, this is never the case. In fact, over the last decade or so, many corporations have brought to the fore the importance of values. How, then, does this vacuuming of personal values take place?

From a corporation's perspective, MBTerror can operate effectively only if the employee's personal self becomes an empty box, i.e., totally devoid of personal values. MBTerror managers therefore tell their staff, even during induction courses, that contact with their personal vision or values (including religious, cultural, spiritual, ethical and ethnic) are irrelevant when it comes to working in the corporation. All that matters is some sort of agreed set of corporate values. The new, imposed values have strong roots and biases. They do not emerge from a void; they come from a corporate elite, with the evident effects on those who experience such values for the first time.

Since corporate values must supersede personal and social values, training is fully devoted to diluting personal values and promoting those advanced by the company. In particular, people are told to embrace personal considerations only outside the work environment. Any gap between a personal and corporate value system is a source of fear. Fear grows by the minute, when, to maintain or advance in their jobs, employees must separate themselves from their personal ethical foundation and join a world whose roots are foreign to them.

Fear arises when fitting in—wholesale adoption of corporate values and beliefs—dominates the work environment and employees have to relegate their belief system to evenings, weekends and holidays. This not only generates fear but also generates major crises of loyalties, particularly in people who have complex, non-mechanical jobs, such as policy formulation or strategic communications. Experience shows that the most affected employees are those who have a clear vision, or a strong set of values related to the issues that are the main object of management.

MBTerror thrives on deepening those crises of loyalties. In some instances, the end result is a strong move towards ideological discrimination and entrenchment. This form of discrimination is so pervasive that it silences those who need the organization most, for instance those who have to stay for the health benefits or for financial reasons. When many people are silenced, especially minorities, yet another form of terror arises.

In the realm of MBTerror, uniform values are much better than diverse values, despite all that it may be said to the contrary. Corporate values become the norm and yardstick against which every person is ultimately evaluated. They become the way to create personal and corporate images of what people are supposed to be.

II. Govern by tight rules to maximize tensions

Proclamation of corporate values is not enough. These values must be translated into incentives, rules and arrangements. The rules must be tight in order to keep people on the tips of their toes and employees must hear them repeatedly. This creates the need for imposing tough corporate discipline that, in the end, may generate higher or lower productivity.

MBTerror demands rules that cannot be violated. Employees report that these tight and exaggerated rules keep everyone tense, as they are continuously reminded that they have to erase their own values and beliefs to succeed in the company. MBTerror uses so many rules that it often eliminates individual initiative and insight and the corporate system operates with a huge degree of arbitrariness. Tight governance is becoming popular in corporations with a lot of cultural diversity, where people are more likely to have different viewpoints on how a corporate culture should look. To avoid debates that may question the corporate culture, managers invoke a large and exhaustive battery of regulations around every task, for instance, highly detailed instructions on how and when to write something (deadlines are a strong source of tension) and how it should be reviewed and finalized.

The only ones who thrive with these rules seem to be those in positions of corporate power—the set of rules reflects their own values—or those who resonate with this type of behavior. In fact, after reviewing the results of psychological tests, it appears that corporations, on average, tend to hire people with the same personality types. The roots of terror are thus reinforced through uniformity in viewpoint as well as the imposition of numerous rules.

III. Link differences of opinion or ideology to individual performance

MBTerror strives to silence people, particularly those who have a perspective that may challenge the present corporate conditions and policies. In fact, we could measure this management system's successful implementation by how effectively fear spreads and becomes deep-rooted in silence. Silencing employees is a powerful management instrument and I have seen it used and practiced openly many times.

To silence people, managers link differences in opinions or ideology to performance assessments, most of them written. Rather than recognize a different way of thinking about an issue or course of action, rather than recognize the existence of relevant or irreconcilable differences in opinion and leave it there, managers simply label an employee a low performer. Since people do not want to be evaluated as low performers, they choose to say nothing, or become yes men. In many ways, MBTerror can have tremendous negative impacts on corporate development, as one or many potentially valuable perspectives are marginalized from the mainstream

In some cases, senior management silences people by promoting them, giving them higher bonuses or salary increases, or sidetracking them into jobs that are not in the mainstream. An excellent title, larger office space, more-than-average material resources and other gadgets may accompany the sidetracking process. However, linking differences in opinions to performance has potentially disastrous consequences for both work satisfaction and personal fulfillment.

Another dimension of this process must be mentioned. Evaluators often put something in writing that differs significantly from what they tell their staff. However, corporate filters are weak, and staff come to know this sooner, rather than later. One of the most pervasive outcomes of this duality between written and oral evaluations is that people never really know why they are not promoted or don't advance in their careers. Part of the secret is to keep negative information in the grapevine without any possibility for staff to discover its origin. The ongoing lack of clarity demoralizes the affected staff members.

IV. Use indifference and behavioral modalities that are erratic and unpredictable

The purposeful adoption of erratic personal or social behavior as a management style constitutes another powerful tool of MBTerror. Since many employees are sensitive to a manager's behavioral changes, some organizations have experts on this particular technique and advise managers on its best use.

As an example, one day a manager may greet his or her peers, while the next day he/she ignores them. The manager does this frequently, particularly during the time of performance evaluations. It creates insecurity, exaggerates the state of play and becomes a totally unpleasant experience for staff members. If an employee is not particularly self-confident, this behavior can terrorize her/him, as the employee most often interprets it as a critical message that the manager intends to bring into the evaluation process.

A manager's failure to respond to an employee's request for a one-to-one meeting is another example of MBTerror behavior. The employee is left in the cold and usually concludes that he/she is not on good terms with the boss. Yet another technique is a manager's rude or even brutal public behavior towards an employee whom the manager knows is weak and cannot counter the attack.

One final example of an MBTerror tool is management pressure on employees not to exercise their civil rights. This might include a demand that they do not join a union, staff association or any other form of organization that may challenge management decisions.

V. Make sure that the feedback to staff is mainly negative.

Negativity is a major form of terror. The more managers apply it, the better it works. Managers who use terror-related management practices apply them particularly to those who have the greatest need for long-term job stability. This strategy essentially translates as: "I am doing good work as a manager, but you, as a staff, are doing a very poor job." The idea here is to establish a distance in performance and/or to create an artificial crisis.

Many times, the negative judgments passed on to staff are not totally related to the job at hand but are more directly related to their personal characteristics. Thus, negativity is spread at the personal level. Being a source of fear is an intrinsic component of the terror-based strategy. It is also important to know that managers mimic their superiors. Thus, it may be possible that managers are a source of fear because their bosses do so too.

VI. Create artificial crises where the manager is the hero.

Many management courses are concerned with corporate culture and how to change it. One of the most well-known techniques to advance cultural change is the creation of an artificial sense of crisis. A crisis of deep proportions is best, as it will make even the strongest persons consider and support the suggested changes. In crisis mode, loyalties get manipulated a great deal.

The problem with this technique is its impure intent and the resultant negative trajectory that rolls out after the crisis. This is particularly the case when, as a result of crisis-inspired, corporate changes, the majority of employees sees that the entrenched power group has consolidated its gains after the artificial crisis is over. This prevents others from advancing within the company as the crisis is resolved. Thus, employees fight to resolve the crisis but do not benefit from winning.

Crises are indeed an instrument of fear, worry and exaggeration, and they produce the necessary institutional spaces to feed terrorist behavior. Those who created the crisis are usually the only ones to benefit from it. Structure-based reorganizations are often preceded by an artificial crisis of some proportions.[30]

VII. Destroy employee self-confidence through the allocation of impossible jobs

Managing by terror necessitates inhibiting grass roots or spontaneous leadership. Otherwise, corporate conditions and actions may be challenged and terror related-activities would then need to be escalated. This escalation is often costly in more than one way: time, money, etc.

MBTerror represents a real threat to those who are innate achievers. Those who have strategically designed, terror-based instruments see these achievers as a big problem. To weaken such leaders, they are given impossible and controversial jobs so that they cannot perform well or they burn themselves out in the process. This technique seems to work wonders with many leaders who, in the end, give in and decide to conform as a mode of survival. However, in the process of conforming, they lose their self-confidence completely.

The process of job allocation is a critical one as far as employee productivity and satisfaction is concerned. Corporate cost-cutting and downsizing have brought a new generation of young professionals with insufficient job experience into the workplace. They are often the first to be assigned the impossible jobs, which they eagerly accept in their desire to be successful. Failure to live up to job expectations can force them into corporate compliance and diminish initiative and originality.

The last two techniques—impossible job assignments and the creation of artificial crises—share a common ingredient: In both cases the managers who apply these techniques come out as heroes. This fosters relationships of dependence and attachment, so that further manipulation may take place.

VIII. Create a group dynamic that perpetuates a continuous crisis of loyalties

The manager who uses MBTerror needs strong alliances to survive. Some are made explicit, but most of them are implicit to avoid a public questioning of corporate favoritism. If you happen to be perceived as belonging to the "other group," you will never get any significant benefits, real promotions, etc.

The members of the corporate elite make many decisions behind closed doors. This is particularly the case with bonuses, merit increases and other salary adjustments. Since employees must never know who actually makes those decisions, those who inquire about pay increases or bonuses often get the answer: "It was a management decision." People from personnel departments often support this process and are the ones who legitimize these management decisions and practices.

If an employee is not among the loyalists, that individual will simply not get where he/she wants to go. Some of those who implement these practices pretend that employees should actually be grateful that they got what they did, "given a number of considerations" (never explained) about their performance.

In many instances, making false charges against staff accelerates a crisis of loyalties. Nobody ever seems to know who made the charges and why they were made. In the language of a friend of mine, "It is the opinion of the choir," though nobody knows who is singing in the choir.

Many other techniques and strategies make MBTerror a success. A manager can share only partial information with an employee, which means that the staff member is always working with an incomplete feasibility set. This can have serious consequences, particularly when a staff member is implementing a delicate and controversial assignment. Finally, a manager might tell an employee that a meeting or conversation is confidential, and then share its content with others.

ACCELERATING A PROCESSES

MBTerror works best during major periods of unemployment. At such times, employees do not have an opportunity to move out and find new jobs and reconcile their loyalties. These techniques also work well during unstable social and political periods. The swing of the political, economic, religious or ethnic pendulum can bring fear and insecurity to those in the opposite camp.

Most corporations develop major supportive mechanisms to keep MBTerror growing swiftly. For instance, a complementary communication strategy creates a reality (or a type of reality) in which opponents become second-class citizens or are portrayed as undeserving of the same respect and attention as the power elite. The spin doctors behind these communication strategies also terrorize people by using false or distorted information that creates an appearance of truth or signifies a situation that would be unacceptable without their influence. Plain lies are also allowed.

No less important, is the misuse of human values that are deeply ingrained in people's belief systems to attain an objective through unacceptable means. This happens often in the public sector. Such terms as freedom, democracy, accountability, transparency, fraternity and many more are exploited to legitimize MBTerror and the cause for which it is fighting. In some cases, millions of innocent people have died or lost their jobs because of MBTerror related activities.

Working in collusion with personnel departments, all these forms a thick cobweb of constantly reinforced corporate or political power. A form of misguided loyalty unfolds in which MBTerror affects personnel department staff. They fear the negative consequences of moving away from the line dictated by management and they themselves become victims of MBTerror.

Managers who use terror commonly promote minorities to do the dirty work. This means that errors, mistakes and the application of MBTerror techniques appear to be executed by people who are not in the entrenched management team. In a form of veiled personal abuse, the people at the lower level receive great benefits to conquer spaces for management that otherwise would expose the managers in question. It is also part of the MBTerror strategy to divide groups at the grassroots level. Using selective methods of rewards, they pit one group against the other, or they purposely fractionalize existing groups to gain or maintain the level of power. In the end, MBTerror propagates more terror, scaling up a disastrous system of management.

WHY DO MANAGERS DO THIS?

It is important to reflect on why a manager does manage in this form. Clearly, once aware of the above-mentioned situations and techniques, reasonable managers will stop doing so.

There is no doubt that many managers could claim ignorance and incompetence. However, it would be rather difficult to convince the people who are managed that managers are ignorant or incompetent and that, as a result, they use terror in their sphere of influence. In many ways, managers are nominated in those positions because they are more competent than others in management. At least, this is the theory behind the promotions.

We would suggest that claiming ignorance or incompetence is too simple of an explanation to address this phenomenon of MBTerror. It is in this vein I would like to offer some other possibilities.

One of them is stress and the fact that many managers are stressed out most of the time. Some are passive receptors of stress and bottle up well, and they distress outside work. It is important to focus on this matter for a moment. Part of their stress at work comes from excessive responsibilities, their inability to manage as some have been promoted without the skills, or because of their stress in their personal life that they carry to their everyday work. Managers have the need to manage both upwards and downwards. Many times, the stress comes from managing upwards, where the manager of the manager is in the end the principal sources of stress. Thus, inside the corporation, one is to analyze the source of stress that comes from managing upwards.

Not less important is the stress managers bring from their own personal life. As human beings, they also have families and the obligations and issues that such a position embodies. In those situations, they are often the managers too, and the provider, leader, educator, coach, friend, father... It is a 24 hours dedication to management.

Yet another factor leading to using terror at the office has its roots in being insecure. Insecure often leads to many forms of behavior and to exacerbate the manager's lack of identity. While this is not a treaty in psychology, it is important to focus on what happens when a manager is insecure. The tendency is to micromanage people, second guess employees, select one or two favorite ones and use them also as instruments of terror and fear, and the like. Managers who are self-confident are often more at ease with themselves and much more patient in accepting errors by those they manage and are not that keen in using to the extreme a "punishment-reward" system. Very seldom such issues are addressed in management training.

Furthermore, managers end up using fear and terror because they are not able or allowed to bring opposite or different values. In particular, to bring the values of love, compassion, caring and sharing, to name a few. These are identified as sources of weaknesses rather than sources of strength. It is difficult to forget the expression 'touchy feely stuff'. This is not allowed in most cases, and when it is done, this is done at the manager's expense! Thus, many managers are living in constant duality between the values they profess inside themselves and what they need to express to attain the goals and objectives they have to attain.

Many of them at home do believe in the powers that come from their inner self, their spirit, their souls and the many instruments available from those realms. However, their ability to express this experience is only relegated for the weekends as it is not possible to integrate these instruments and values in the daily work.

Also, terror and fear are also practiced, because other managers – who are successful ones—practice such a style. This is a snowball effect in management as managers watch other managers and their careers very closely.

Finally, and as difficult it is to express this, fear and terror happens because many managers are psychologically unstable. They use the same style at home with their spouses and children, and so on. Once a person is an abuser, it tends to be like that everywhere. There are reasons linked to their childhood, or even previous lives. Here, the key to such management style is inner anger, which is frequently expressed in the various techniques discussed above. Inner anger is latent, and it expresses itself in sophisticated and intelligent ways. Terror is practiced as an outgrowth of frustration that is born from inner anger.

Of all the above, one important message is to be kept in mind: the behavior of managers is a composite of what is happening within the corporation and their own private lives. It is also a composite of what appears on the external environment as well as their inner self. Managers are indeed normal human beings who have the problems and challenges everyone has in life. Therefore, to change the present situation, it is essential to look far beyond behavior and what is seen as an external dimension of managers.

SELF-REALIZED ENTREPRENEURSHIP

Many people ask whether a good manager is something innate or something that one could become. Not an easy question although I believe that it is possible to be a good manager, or at least a better manager, out of learning how to address the above. This is also an important issue in that it creates an enabling environment to improve the state of play in many corporations with the people they have at the top.

However, human transformation is an elaborate process, particularly for those who are not the innate ones. I used to say to my children: if you have to be good at it, you have to work at it". But the notion of 'work' was not just something at the surface. This is extremely well known by athletes. It is not just a matter of techniques and practice, notwithstanding the importance of both. It is the embodiment within yourself of "that" one is supposed to do. Your inner self and the very subtle and intricate aspects of oneself are in the end the difference between the best athlete and just a good one. When one sees a violin player at its best, it is clear that it is not just technique and practice. They become the music itself. They self-realize in themselves the music they are playing.

Thus, the key is not the having, doing or knowing. The key to management is also "becoming".

A good example of the above is related to the notion of entrepreneurship.

In the past, major emphasis has been placed on business entrepreneurship for managers. Experts in this area know a lot about costs, finances, strategic planning, marketing and the like. They represent management guided by knowledge as an external ingredient.

Because the realities facing corporations have dramatically changed, some are now suggesting a focus on social entrepreneurship. Social entrepreneurs are sensitive to and aware of the social environment within which the corporation develops. This is important, as corporations are not isolated entities. They exist in social environments that they modify, or which modify them. However, knowledge and awareness of the social environment are not enough.

However, the ultimate form of management must be embedded in people who have become themselves as fully realized and conscious beings. This may be called "spiritual entrepreneurship." Today, managers are frequently selected through an advocacy process. As this is not sufficient to become a self-realized person one needs to create the necessary conditions in the corporate world that support the selection of managers who, along with their professional abilities, have the ability to self-realize corporate and personal values. Again, these values are not just as words or advocacy in communication strategies, but as the violinist, they are to become fully embodied into those values.

In the end, the key to be a good manager is to be a self-realized human being. To embed what you preach. To be the values you want the corporation to advocate. And, this process of transformation by necessity involves the development of a person's inner self. As it was stated above, to get rid of anger one must be able to embody peace in its totality. One needs to transform oneself to create the space for the self-realization of peace. And, this applies to all the other values and situations.

This is why it is important to state that the future of most corporations will rest on the hiring of self-realized beings. There is a need for managers and workers who not only reject terror and violence but who are such that the terror and violence are not part of their total life settings. These are the self-realized managers.

The notion of self-realized managers is not yet in management and entrepreneurship. These self-realized managers will perform extremely well in problem solving as well as in predicting the future. These are two essential functions of managers. It is central that a major attention be given to the ability, for example, to become the other without losing one's own identity and manage that person properly. Inner development is at the core of the self-realized manager and it is probably the only form of human transformation to make one the best manager. It is evident that the consciousness of a self-realized manager would be high and, therefore, she/he can resolve real problems in humane ways. He/she can also predict the future accurately, so that a corporation and its employees greatly benefit from corporate actions and behavior.

SOME IMPORTANT STEPS

Transformation into a good manager and away from MBTerror will require some important dimensions and practical steps. Eliminating terror in the corporate life will not be easy because it will require also the inner transformation of existing managers and those managers to be. But it is not an impossible task.

Herewith a few suggestions that may eventually form the basis of an agenda for action.

First, understand that corporate values are not just words that are to be advocated to create a corporate image or something similar. The good managers will also embody those values in real life, like the violinist embodies the music that she/he is supposed to play. Otherwise, managers will have no credibility to lead corporations. Corporate values, management values, human and spiritual values are to be fully experienced and owned internally. They cannot remain in the abstract or just an object of advocacy. The introduction of morals, ethics and humanistic values necessitates a process of inner transformation.

Second, eliminate all forms of violence, be it explicit, implicit, overt or veiled. This requires a discipline that goes far beyond having technical knowledge. It demands a new corporate soul, a new modus vivendi, a new set of goals and clearly demarcated processes and procedures. It involves not only one manager, but all managers, staff. Here staff related organizations, like unions or other forms of association must be fully involved.

Third, the solution(s) to all of the above goes (go) far beyond creating or imposing yet another style of management. The reason is simple: MBT affects the soul of the manager and the souls of the people that she/he manages. The solution must therefore also be found within our inner self. The replacement of styles of management does not necessarily leads to human transformation. Thus, the same managers, at the same level of consciousness and coherence, will again fault within the new style of management.

Fourth, the ultimate inner change for managers and corporations, and the ultimate healing process for those who have been badly affected by MBT, lie in a spiritual process of human transformation: to embody inside oneself "all dimensions of management." Thus, if a corporate value is compassion, then managers and staff must have had the outer and inner experience of compassion. Otherwise, it is only advocacy for the sake of advocacy. As stated earlier, in the case of human and corporate values, these values are not just words, but specific forms of human reality (states of being), individual and collective states of being. Thus, compassion demands to be compassionate. To actually manage with the intent to create human security in those one manages, managers and staff must self-realize the state of security.

Fifth, management is not a theoretical proposition. Management is a practice, and as such, it is part of that practice to attain levels of human transformation that are coherent with the purposes and aims at hand. Management is to manage, an active form of human transformation.

In essence, the transformation to new forms of management demands that we move from the business manager to the social manager (one who self-realizes the contexts of business) and, furthermore, it demands that we move from the social manager to the spiritual or conscious manager. Here, spiritual means a transformation that is embodied deeply in the managers themselves.

What has often been referred here as a self-realized manager. This is to say, a self-realized being, a person who has already experienced the full dimensions of the values, instruments and practices that she/he is promoting as the ethos of any new management style.

Miscellaneous Aspects: At a Glance

Each manager could add many more ways and means to structure new forms of human transformation in the corporate world and within the realms of their own personal lives.

It is clear within this context that to become a good manager is a process and not just a title. Many good people are in the wrong positions as there was not another avenue for promotion and internal recognition, both materially and socially. Thus, these people accepted a position of management for a higher salary, for example, and entered processes of transformation that make them insecure, stressed, and the like. The recipe for terror and bad management practices.

In addition, the process of transformation that managers go through in the corporation's world really affects the personal life and the family life of managers. Therefore, what is outlined here should also be of interest to spouses, children, relatives and friends. Sometimes, violence at home is the result of the transformational process the managers go through at the corporate level! Many, to soften the situation, turn into alcoholism, eating disorders, and other manifestations of inner anxieties.

The world depends on what corporations are doing today. In turn, it is incumbent upon us to take care of the managers and workers. As a co-equal world citizen, we all must care and take care of them. This is not just dollars and cents. It is a fundamental pillar to construct a new destiny for our children and future generations.

Terror can be reduced, and it must be eliminated as a form of management. In the immediate, one should begin by changing the language of management, as there are many terms that are or insinuate some form of terror and violence, or create fear (sometimes, purposely so). This change in language will be a tough thing to do, as fads and traditions dominate this language. One example is that of doing the 'dirty work' for top managers. Who is to do the dirty work? Why should it be dirty in the first place?

In the end, management has become a public good, as the managerial decisions affect us all. There is nothing impermeable about corporations anymore. MBTerror affects the health of employees, who in turn use their health insurance to the limits to cope with the impacts of such terror. This response affects the insurance premiums of everyone in the system and not just those in the said corporation. Thus, the nature of management as a public good.

FINAL THOUGHTS

Corporations are entities of human beings and thus an incubator for different forms of human transformation and self-realization. They are not atomized buildings and machineries. They are no more and no less than those who own, work for and manage them. Thus, they have a soul. Their products embody imprints, the spirit, intents and actions of those who belong to that corporation. Their clients are human beings and the external impacts of corporations and management actions greatly affect the human and natural environments.

Corporations are like human bodies, with parts, dimensions and functions that are complex and need to be understood in both their material and non-material existences. Thus, the style of management adopted will greatly determine corporate internal and external behavior and results.

MBTerror is not only unacceptable, but it is also shortsighted and destructive. To move away from this style of management is not trivial. It will not happen by fiat. It will happen by creating the conditions for a form of human transformation that is not violent, full of fear, and terror.

The process of inner human transformation advocated here is essential as, in truth; any management style is likely to contain an element of terror, as our human world is governed by relativism. Therefore, there is always an unenlightened side of management, in whatever style one is willing to promote. This unenlightened dimension of management comes from the level of consciousness of managers and staff.

Styles of management cannot be understood in a vacuum of mechanical rules and procedures. Rules and procedures are formulated, developed and applied by managers. Their content and implementation perfectly reflect the consciousness of corporate managers and leaders.

A new corporation must emerge in this world, and this is only possible based on a new process of human transformation that will lead to a higher level of human consciousness. It is this new consciousness the center stage of human transformation and change that also permeates corporate life and behavior. A new world needs a new corporation.

EPILOGUE

"Truth is not something outside to be discovered, it is something inside to be realized." —**Osho**

"He is richest who is content with the least, for content is the wealth of nature." —**Socrates**

"I have learned over the years that when one's mind is made up, this diminishes fear; knowing what must be done does away with fear." —**Rosa Parks**

"If you want to build a ship, don't drum up people together to collect wood and don't assign them tasks and work, but rather teach them to long for the endless immensity of the sea." —**Antoine de Saint-Exupéry**

The severe acute respiratory syndrome coronavirus 2 (SARS-CoV-2) and its connected COVID-19 infectious disease brought the world to a screeching halt. It changed our daily life. The pandemic has challenged leadership at many levels testing the value priorities and decisions for people or for profit, for short term fixes or long-term solutions. It has put to test the willingness and abilities of leaders to prescribe policies and course of actions based on science and data or political and economic interests. These dualities are not new as we think about the climate crisis and how political and economic leaders have been ignoring scientific data regarding the threat that climate change has on the health of the planet and our very survival as human beings. More studies are emerging showing that even pandemics have direct correlations to climate change, deforestation and other preexisting conditions due to long-term exposure to air pollution and exposure to fine particulate matter emissions.

We know that pandemics such as the coronavirus may occur more often with the persistence of those climate conditions as warming and changing weather will shift the vectors and spreads of disease. We know that methane emissions, largely due to factory farming, will generate faster-mutating and more virulent pathogens. We know that if future leaders want to seriously address the prevention and preparation for the next pandemic, they will need to factor climate change mitigation targets and solutions. The Sustainable Development Goals and SDG 13 on climate action which center around the important commitments as in the 2015 Paris Agreement are fundamental steps and strategies for reversing the course and initiating a path for healing the planet. However, we also know that these new directions and course of actions will not be possible unless a new level of consciousness as sensitivity to our interconnectedness is rediscovered and properly articulated in our actions and decisions.

The arguments, models and reflections offered in this book have tried to help us all go deeper in the conversations toward sustainability and leadership by integrating, articulating and discovering what "consciousness" means for each of us. Unconscious leaders will simply ignore the scientific evidence and continue with a status quo for short term convenient solutions. Sometimes they will even instill an administration of management-by-terror to continue its imposed powers. Leaders who embrace these concepts of consciousness and interconnectedness will be part of a new generation of leaders. One that will lead humanity to new horizons for eco-logical relations based on shared global responsibility and 'ethicnomics'. We have examined how these new types of leaders share different levels of ethical sensitivity and collective emotions; they reflect the directions and depth of a new paradigm based on sustainability values and sustainable development competencies. They reflect an interdisciplinary mindset, capable of integrating humanity with ecology, the arts with science and poetry with technology. They will be able to understand sustainability beyond a green concern and are connected to all aspects of our social, natural, economic, political, cultural as well as personal, collective and institutional systems.

Sustainable development is not just an addition to a given economic system, such as the neoliberal system. It is a fundamental new paradigm that embraces a vision of humanity in complete harmony with nature. It is a paradigm that recognizes human beings as an integral part of an immense matrix of different forms of conscious life. It is a paradigm that demands a new construct, not only the field of economics, but also encompassing political, social, institutional and cultural elements. It affects and transforms every aspect of human activity.

As such, sustainable development demands new policies, programs and projects, in conjunction with institutional and social reforms, in order to attain a proper balance between human needs and the whole carrying capacity of the planet. Yet, it is even more than that. Sustainable development heightens the need to pay attention to the material as well as the non-material (spiritual) dimensions of the welfare of all beings and of all forms of life. Sustainable development demands a new leader and a new form of leadership, which pays attention to the inner and outer ecology of all forms of life.

Therefore, these forms of leadership for sustainable development must surface today to embrace two fundamental realities: (i) that sustainable development does not only possess a physical dimension (it is not just a material phenomenon) and (ii) that the planet earth is not just a material thing; it is a live being. Understanding these propositions is not just a matter of faith, but a matter of a profound human experience. Both propositions bring to the fore the critical role that "human consciousness" plays in the formation of leaders as well as in the interdependent inclusion of all sentient beings and nature. Leadership must be understood as a collective phenomenon, i.e., the human collective and the natural collective. It is this collective experience which connects all forms of consciousness and all forms of life.

It is this understanding that gave form to a Consciousness Sustainable Leadership Paradigm (CSL). This paradigm distills the unique attributes of "the conscious leader" we all need now in the world. These attributes are not just universal in nature (e.g., patient, committed, resilient), but these are also very unique attributes born out of the view one holds on the real meaning of sustainable development.

Universities must change their approach to leadership formation and their understanding of leadership because sustainable development is a level of consciousness, a bundle of rights, a style of life, and a collection of values. This view is a radical departure from paradigms of leadership that have adopted very traditional definitions of sustainability, even including the so-called SDGs by the United Nations.

The solutions to the ecological crisis we live today (e.g., pandemics, global warming, climate change, biodiversity depletion) will be found by attaining a new level of collective human consciousness. The old consciousness that has created these problems does not have the mechanism to resolve it. A level of consciousness that will bring to the fore the importance of "interdependence" in all its forms: among human beings and between human beings and all forms of life. Without this understanding, we will never attain the objectives and goals of sustainable development.

Alfredo's Epilogue: Marco and I walked through the Muir Woods National Monument, where the coastal red wood sequoias are mighty witnesses of the most sacred power of life on this planet. It is difficult to imagine that those very ancient trees do not have energy, memory, intelligence, and consciousness. Certainly, it was not my experience. Also, to have learned that the founders of the United Nations visited that park 75 years ago, it was a clear message to me that everyone understood the need for establishing a unique, sustainable, and harmonious life style on this planet, for the welfare of human beings, sentient beings and nature. It also confirmed that the most profound relationship with the earth is seating on the throne of universal wisdom. Thus, it won't just be 'hope' that will drive us towards the self-realization, conservation, and respect of each and every dimension of life. We are planetary citizens and, as such, we must understand that we are not the center or the sole reason, attention and action as regards life in all its expressions. Inclusion of all beings and nature forms the foundation of our collective moral responsibility: A New Eco-Morality. Future leaders must be embedded in this New Eco-Morality.

A true holistic view of the relationship between humans and nature needs to emerge not from the mind or the ego, but from a much higher state of individual and collective consciousness. To transcend the inadequate state of present reality, these expressions are not just a cliché, or an instrument of speech; they are the foundations of the necessary space that would define a very specific and concrete spiritual path that we must follow. It is this path that will enable leaders to self-realize that nature is a "living being", and not just as a "thing". That will be the moment when we all could proclaim the real and holistic meaning of life. This must transcend us as individuals and, therefore, it must permeate all aspects of public life— government, economy, institutions, business and citizenship. This is the core defining new forms of leadership.

In this spiritual path, we will realize that everyone and every being possesses a universal, unchanged, and fully developed essence, and life expression, on this planet, and our main responsibility and purpose is to discover that essence. This process goes beyond thinking, learning, doing, having or behaving. It is a profound inner reality of the being and becoming, which houses the source of all wisdoms that condition all possible courses of action, behavior, habits, mindset, etc. This inner reality is present in all forms of life. This pure essence of life is in constant interaction with the purest source of consciousness and wisdom, from where leaders need to operate from. Some call it our Divine Self. Others call it our Buddha Mind. However, for the moment, it seems that this unique inner reality is like a dirty mirror, we shall clean a million times from our attachments, power-seeking, materialism, greed, fear, ego... Education and leadership demand a constant cleaning of this mirror –individual and collective mirror-- to bring about the right vision and actions for the benefit of all. Therefore, leadership is, in essence, a process of self-realization, and not just habits, attitudes, perceptions, attributes, behavior. A true leader must unfold from this process of cleaning his/her own mirror.

Marco's Epilogue: During the development of this book, I spent a beautiful sunny day walking with Alfredo in the Marin Headlands overlooking the beautiful Pacific Ocean. I shared with him my view of our existence and how it inspires my life. I used the analogy of light to express the deeper meaning of our existence. First, we are all like rays of light. The idea of a ray of light is important because it gives light to objects and gives warmth and energy to situations. The value and identity of that ray of light is independent from its actual accomplishments. It is valuable as an expression of the start that emanated from it. Its existence is not just limited to its mission and trajectory but to its belonging to the star not only in its origins but also "at the end" of its journey. Light and energy are known realities to our level of knowledge that represent something deeper and ontologically different in our experiences of life and existence. The other components of the universe called "dark matter", "dark energy" are other elements that we know that they are there but that are fully explained or understood in our current level of knowledge. Light and energy are symbolic expressions of alternative dimensions that we are all familiar with but cannot fully explain such as love and intimacy, justice and truth, care and respect. Although we all have some experience of these dimensions in our human existence, we may have different level of consciousness on their significance. Second, love transcends our current existence. Love is what ultimately best represents dimensions that transcend time, space and current experience or life. It may sound too poetic to some as love has been used in many ways, but it surely carries a significance beyond current living existence. Love is ultimately behind what we have attempted to explain around the notion of consciousness. True self-less, collective, and universal love relates and transcends our leadership call and our interconnected sustainability experience and responsibility. The pathways and notions highlighted in this book for understanding conscious sustainability leadership are like rays of light to discover and realize our own deeper identities as parts of the whole.

ENDNOTES

1. Dale Carnegie's prescriptions in his *How to Win Friends and Influence People* is centered on a principle that is a variation of the Golden Rule: "treat others as you would like to be treated." While this early approach of leadership was oversimplified, its message represented a significant departure and evolution from the previously known leadership model of coercion (authoritarian leadership) or reward-for-desired-behavior approach (transactional leadership). Through these earlier developments, leader-behavior emerged as distinguished from boss-behaviors and began seeking approaches centered on values and mission (transformational leadership) and service (servant leadership). For a good overview of the evolution of leadership theories see Northouse, P. G. (2019). *Leadership: Theory and practice*. SAGE.

2. Michael Shinagel, "The Paradox of Leadership," Harvard University, Division of Continuing Education, December 9, 2019, https://www.extension.harvard.edu/professional-development/blog/paradox-leadership

3. Joe Iarocci, "Why are There so Many Leadership Books? Here Are 5 Reasons," Carnway, October 26, 2015, https://serveleadnow.com/why-are-there-so-many-leadership-books/

4. Peter Bregman, "Why So Many Leadership Programs Ultimately Fail," Harvard Business Review, July 10, 2013, https://hbr.org/2013/07/why-so-many-leadership-program

5. Bregman, 2013.

6. Pope Francis, Encyclical Letter Laudato Si'of The Holy Father Francis On Care for Our Common Home, No. 86. Citation from Catechism of the Catholic Church,340, 24 May 2015, http://www.vatican.va/content/francesco/en/encyclicals/documents/papa-francesco_20150524_enciclica-laudato-si.html#_ftnref63

7.   Pine, Red. 2013. The Lankavatara Sutra: Translation and Commentary. XLI, 133. http://www.vlebooks.com/vleweb/product/openreader?id=none&isbn=97816 19020368.

8.   Interdisciplinarity in academia is a debated subject in creation of knowledge (research), as well as in the theoretical applications (teaching) and the discoveries and promotion of new realities (service). Interdisciplinarity encompasses other correlated related concepts as trans-disciplinarity, pluri-disciplinarity, and multi-disciplinarity. Many intellectual, social, and practical problems require interdisciplinary approaches as reality reflects complex phenomena in society, nature, economy, etc. The Greeks and Romans first, and later the polymath geniuses of the Renaissance employed interdisciplinary solutions to complex problems. Sustainable development is in itself an interdisciplinary subject in academia as it deals with problems requiring analysis and synthesis across economic, social and environmental spheres. Read more about interdisciplinarity in academia in Nissani, M. (1997). "Ten cheers for interdisciplinarity: The Case for Interdisciplinary Knowledge and Research". Social Science Journal. 34 (2): 201-216. doi:10.1016/S0362-3319(97)90051-3

9.   The holistic view of our interconnected lives on earth are symbolically represented in the first Earth images of space. The first, called Earthrise, came on Christmas Eve 1968 when astronaut William Anders saw "Spaceship Earth" with his fellow crewmen as they circled the Moon on Apollo 8, the first manned spacecraft to leave the Earth's orbit. The second came, called The Blue Marble, came from the 1972 Apollo 16. These images affected the history of human culture and influenced our perception of Earth as a whole planet, a Gaia interconnected living organism. See James Lovelock's Gaia Hypotheses (or theory). J. E. Lovelock (1972). "Gaia as seen through the atmosphere". Atmospheric Environment. 6 (8): 579–580. doi:10.1016/0004-6981(72)90076-5

10. The "I Am Because You Are" notion is also about the interconnected existence expressed in the ancient African concept of Ubuntu that has played in Nelson Mandela's leadership for a post-apartheid South Africa. Oppenheim, Claire E. "Nelson Mandela and the power of Ubuntu." Religions 3, no. 2 (2012): 369-388.

11. The Human Factor is a concept studied and applied in medicine among other disciplines. "Human factors is concerned with applying what is known about human behavior, abilities, limitations, and other characteristics to the

design of systems, tasks/activities, environments, and equipment/technologies. It is also concerned with the design of training programs and instructional materials that support the performance of tasks or the use of technology/equipment." National Research Council. (2011). Health care comes home: the human factors. National Academies Press. Available at https://www.nap.edu/read/13149/chapter/5

12. 'Empowerment' expands on the notion of 'development' by going beyond the economic aspect of growth and integrating a set of dimensions and processes (capabilities) designed to increase the degree of autonomy and self-determination in people and in communities. Noble Laureate Amartya Sen had defined empowerment as a capability approach that provides not only a framework for evaluating human welfare (HDI, human development index), but a tool for advancing it through a sustainable human development process. The empowerment process goes beyond economic, social, political, cultural or gender-based solutions. It is also expressed as legal empowerment as a key strategy for poverty eradication and the promotion of inclusive, equitable, and more sustainable livelihoods. See Amartya Sen (2001) Development as freedom. Oxford: Oxford University Press. See also: Marianne Hill (2003) development as Empowerment, Feminist Economics, 9:2-3, 117-135, DOI: 10.1080/1354570022000077962

13. This interconnected paradigm of "conscious development" reflects what indigenous communities in the Americas call "Sumaq Kawsay" often translated as Buen Vivir, right living, a well-being reflecting a respectful co-existence with Mother Earth (nature, directions, space) and the ancestral spirits (co-existence, dimensions, time).

14. For a good overview of Corporate Social Responsibility (CSR) see Rasche, A., Morsing, M., & Moon, J. (Eds.). (2017). Corporate social responsibility: Strategy, communication, governance. Cambridge University Press. See also: Idowu, S. O., Mermod, A. Y., & Kasum, A. S. (2014). People, Planet and Profit: Socio-Economic Perspectives of CSR. Routledge.

15. Read more and explore the resources provided by the UNESCO's Partner Networks drive implementation of the Global Action Programme (GAP) on Education for Sustainable Development (ESD) at https://en.unesco.org/themes/education-sustainable-development

16. Read more and connect with the network of the UNAI at https://academicimpact.un.org/

17. The UNGC-PRME initiative PRME is governed by a Steering Committee representing the UN Global Compact with the main business school accreditation bodies and specialized regional associations such as AACSB, EFMD, AMBA, CEEMAN, AABS, CLADEA, ABIS, ACBSP, and GRLI. Read more at https://www.unprme.org/

18. The Sharing Information on Progress (SIP) is a voluntary reporting that shows the dynamic, diverse, and perhaps also dispersed levels and priorities of responses of connected academic institutions and programs in the way they perceive their alignment with these principles and goals.

19. The Higher Education Sustainability Initiative (HESI) includes about 300 universities committed to projects aligned with the Sustainable Development Goals (SDGs). HESI is a partnership between United Nations Department of Economic and Social Affairs, UNESCO, United Nations Environment, UN Global Compact's Principles for Responsible Management Education (PRME) initiative, United Nations University (UNU), UN-HABITAT, UNCTAD and UNITAR, was created in 2012 in the run-up to the United Nations Conference on Sustainable Development (Rio+20). Read more at https://sustainabledevelopment.un.org/sdinaction/hesi

20. The Catholic philosophical perspectives presented by Pierre de Chardin and Jacques Maritain are quite relevant to understand the foundation and further explore our conversions on conscious sustainability leadership. On one hand, de Chardin in his works on The Phenomenon of Man and The Divine Milieu, he attempted to make sense of the universe by interprets complexity as the axis of evolution of matter (geosphere and biosphere) into consciousness (in human beings), and then to supreme consciousness (the Omega Point). On the other hand, Maritain in his arguments based on Aristotle, Aquinas, and the Thomistic views of critical realism as metaphysic prior to epistemology, integral humanism for political leadership, and his ethical norms rooted in human nature greatly influenced his contributions to the drafting of the United Nations' Universal Declaration of Human Rights (UN-UDHR).

21. #FridaysForFuture is a movement that began in August 2018, after 15-year-old Greta Thunberg and other young activists sat in front of the Swedish parliament. The Fire Drill Friday is a Jane Fonda led movement inspired by Greta Thunberg when she said, "Our House Is on Fire", and we need to act like it. Read more at https://fridaysforfuture.org/ and https://firedrillfridays.com/

22. See this and the complete list of must-read books and publications in the Bibliography section. See a more complete list of sustainability publications and sustainability leaders at https://www.sdg.services/expert-leaders.html

23. The World Social Forum (WSF), which started in Porto Alegre, Brazil in 2001, is an annual gathering of global civil society organizations bringing together NGOs, advocacy groups and formal / informal social movement seeking alternative economic models that reflect the social and environmental values of sustainability. It is meant to be an alternative global proposition to those of the World Economic Forum (WEF) in Davos, Switzerland. The 9th World Social Forum in the Amazon rainforest (Belém) on January 27-February 1, 2009 gathered about 1,900 indigenous people representing 190 ethnic groups who raised the issue of being stateless peoples seeking alternative economic, social and environmental paradigms in line with their cultural and ancestral values.

24. See Tavanti, M. and Sfeir-Younis, A. (2013). Human Rights Based Sustainable Development: Essential Frameworks for an Integrated Approach. The International Journal of Sustainability Policy and Practices 8(3), 21-35. Available at http://ijspp.cgpublisher.com/product/pub.274/prod.38

25. See a description of the exhibit "FEAR: A German State of Mind? at https://www.hdg.de/en/haus-der-geschichte/exhibitions/fear-a-german-state-of-mind

26. There are several studies describing and analyzing the Buddhist paradigms for leadership and for ecology. Here are a few resources that could be used to further explore the literature: Gallagher, D. R. (2012). Environmental Leadership: A Reference Handbook. United Kingdom: SAGE Publications; Buddhist Approach to Global Leadership and Shared Responsibilities for Sustainable Societies (2019). Vietnam: Religion Publisher; The World Is One Flower: Buddhist Leadership for Peace. (2006). United States: Blue Pine.

27. Dasadhamma Sutta: Discourse on The Ten Dhammas" (AN 10.48), translated from the Pali by Piyadassi Thera. Access to Insight (BCBS Edition), 30 November 2013, http://www.accesstoinsight.org/tipitaka/an/an10/an10.048.piya.html .

28. Other useful lists of leadership styles can be explored at Indeed Career Guide at https://www.indeed.com/career-advice/career-development/10-

common-leadership-styles and Icebreaker Ideas at
https://icebreakerideas.com/leadership-styles/

29.   The term "decent" does not intend to convey just a moral stand (though
      morals are important), but the sort of work environment (including human
      rights) that would lead towards human betterment. The International Labor
      Organization (ILO) has recently defined the term "decent work" and those
      interested should study the term and its policy implications.

30.   We are not suggesting that all crises are artificial. Terror is also exercised in
      situations of true crisis.

BIBLIOGRAPHY
TO KNOW MORE

Must Know Readings on Consciousness Leadership

Barrett, R. (2011). *The New Leadership Paradigm: Leading Self, Leading Others, Leading an Organization, Leading in Society.* Lulu.

Bowman, C., Bowman, S., & Douglas, G. M. (2015). *Conscious Leadership: The key to Unlocking Success.* Access Consciousness Publishing.

Carlson, F. (2015). *Conscious Leadership in Action.* Panoma Press.

Crick, F. (1995). *Astonishing Hypothesis: The Scientific Search for the Soul.* Scribner.

Dennett, D. C. (1993). *Consciousness Explained.* Penguin.

Dennett, D. C. (2015). *Content and Consciousness.* Routledge.

Dethmer, J., Chapman, D., & Klemp, K. (2015). *The 15 commitments of conscious leadership: A new paradigm for sustainable success.* Booknook.

Gin, F.K. (2017). *The Sustainability Leader in You.* International Institute for Learning.

Godfrey-Smith, P. (2016). *Other minds: The octopus, the sea, and the deep origins of consciousness.* Farrar, Straus and Giroux.

Hayden, G. (2016). *Becoming A Conscious Leader: How to LeadSuccessfully in a World That's Waking Up.* Panacea Books.

Kofman, F. (2013). *Conscious Business: How to Build Value Through Values.* Sounds True.

Lao Tzu (2006). *Tao Te Ching.* Perennial Classics. Harper.

McIntosh, S. (2015). *Integral Consciousness and the Future of Evolution.* Paragon House.

Searle, J. R., Dennett, D. C., & Chalmers, D. J. (1997). *The mystery of consciousness.* New York Review of Books.

Van Lommel, L. (2010). *Consciousness Beyond Life.* HarperCollins.

Must Know Readings on Sustainability Leadership

Avery, G. C., & Bergsteiner, H. (2012). *Sustainable leadership: Honeybee and locust approaches.* Routledge.

Ducheyne, D. (2017*). Sustainable Leadership: How to Lead in a VUCA World.* Die Keure Publishing.

Laszlo, C., & Cescau, P. (2017). *Sustainable value: How the world's leading companies are doing well by doing good.* Routledge.

Lefko, M. (2017). *Global sustainability: 21 leading CEOs show how to do well by doing good.* Morgan James Publishing.

Marshall, J., Coleman, G., & Reason, P. (2011). *Leadership for Sustainability: An Action Research Approach.* Routledge.

McKibben, B. (2007). *Deep economy: The wealth of communities and the durable future.* Macmillan.

Parkin, S. (2010). *The positive deviant: Sustainability leadership in a perverse world.* Routledge.

Schein, S. (2017). *A new psychology for sustainability leadership: The hidden power of ecological worldviews.* Routledge.

Steffen, S. L., Rezmovits, J., Trevenna, S., & Rappaport, S. (2019). *Evolving leadership for collective wellbeing: Lessons for implementing the United Nations sustainable development goals.* Emerald.

Tsao, F. C., & Laszlo, C. (2019). *Quantum Leadership: New Consciousness in Business.* Stanford University Press.

Must Know Readings on Sustainability

Breen, B., & Hollender, J. (2010). *The Responsibility Revolution: How the Next Generation of Businesses Will Win.* Jossey-Bass.

Brundtland, G. H. and World Commission on Environment and Development. (1987). *Our Common Future (Brundtland Report).* United Nations, Oxford University Press.

Carson, R. (2002-1962). *Silent spring.* Mariner Books

Elkington, J. (1998). *Cannibals with Forks: The Triple Bottom Line of 21st Century Business.* Wiley.

Fuller, R. B. (1968). *Operating Manual for Spaceship Earth*. The Estate of R. Buckminster Fuller.

Gore, A. (2008). *Our Choice: A Plan to Solve the Climate Crisis*. Rodale Books.

Hardin, G. (1968). The Tragedy of the Commons. *Science*, 162(3859), 1243–1248.

Hawken, P., Lovins, A. B., & Lovins, L. H. (1999). *Natural Capitalism: Creating the Next Industrial Revolution*. Routledge.

Leonard, A. (2010). *The Story of Stuff: How Our Obsession with Stuff Is Trashing the Planet, Our Communities, and Our Health-and a Vision for Change*. Free Press.

Lovelock, J. (1979). *Gaia: A New Look at Life on Earth*. OUP Oxford.

McDonough, W., & Braungart, M. (2010). *Cradle to cradle: Remaking the way we make things*. North Point.

Meadows, D. H., Meadows, D. L., Randers, J., Behrens, W. W., & Club de Rome. (1972). *The limits to growth: A report for the Club of Rome's project on the predicament of mankind*.

Pope Francis (2015). *Laudato Si: On Care for Our Common Home*.

Schumacher, E. F. (1973). *Small Is Beautiful: Economics as if People Mattered*.

United Nations. (2002). *Global challenge, global opportunity: Trends in sustainable development. The World Summit on Sustainable Development: the Johannesburg Conference*.

United, Nations. (1992). *Earth Summit, Agenda 21: Programme of Action for Sustainable Development.* The Final Text of Agreements, United Nations Conference on Environment and Development (UNCED) 3-14th June 1992, Rio de Janeiro, Brazil.

Werbach, A. (2009). *Strategy for Sustainability: A Business Manifesto.*

ABOUT THE AUTHORS

Alfredo Sfeir-Younis, Ph.D.

 Dr. Alfredo Sfeir-Younis is a Chilean economist, spiritual leader and healer. He has a Doctorate from the University of Wisconsin in resource economics and international trade and finance. President of the Zambuling Institute for Human Transformation. Sfeir-Younis had a twenty-nine-year career at the World Bank where he was hired as the first environmental economist in 1976 and, later, was appointed Director of the World Bank Office in Geneva, Switzerland. He served as Special Representative to the United Nations and the World Trade Organization from 1996 to 2003. In both institutions he worked in the general fields of human rights, peace, and social justice; within this broader context he initiated and promoted policy in such areas as poverty eradication, international trade and finance, financing of development, indigenous people, gender and women's issues, trade and development, role of indigenous peoples, sustainable management of forestry and fisheries, water management and irrigation, desertification, biodiversity, culture and spirituality in sustainable development, and alternative medicine. A coach and advisor to many leaders around the world.

Marco Tavanti, Ph.D.

 Dr. Marco Tavanti is an Italian Sociologist with over 30 years of experience working for sustainable development and poverty alleviation projects in Europe, East Africa, Latin America, North America and Southeast Asia. He is CEO of SDG-services, President of Sustainable Capacity International SCI-Institute, and co-founder of the World Engagement Institute. He is Professor of Nonprofit Management and Global Leadership at University of San Francisco and serves as a sustainable development and indigenous rights expert for the United Nations and other international organizations. His scholarship explores and promotes cross-cultural, anti- corruption and sustainability in relation to the UN Global Compact and the Principles of Responsible Management Education.

Made in the USA
Columbia, SC
24 September 2020